A Personal Faith Journey

Little Miracles Reveal an Amazing God

Terrence J. Hatch

1

*

Dedications

I dedicate this book first to those who have experienced some of the events. That is especially true of my wife Brenda, and our sons Jonathan, Justin, and Daniel, and our daughters-in-law, Kiley and Paige. I am hoping that by immortalizing these memories we will never forget how amazing God has been.

I also dedicate this book to extended family and friends, and to all future generations of all of the above whose curiosity may lead them to want to know more about their spiritual heritage. And finally I dedicate this book to any and all who might venture into these pages. My prayer is that what you read here might become a catalyst for a deeper and more meaningful relationship with the Creator, both now and for eternity.

* * *

*

4

TABLE OF CONTENTS

INTRODUCTION

You are not reading this by accident. God is offering you the gift of faith, and he has a plan for your life. Even now, he is putting pieces of the puzzle into place that will incredibly make a way for you. Just the fact you stumbled upon this book is a sign that the God of the universe, who controls every molecule, atom, and quark, has a place for you in his plan. This book contains some of the reasons I can make such bold statements in confidence.

Yes, I know such a view raises deep theological questions on mornings when the car won't start or a child is sick. Yet it does not change the facts. I have to believe that there are answers to the tough questions in eternity, simply because God has given us gifts of faith in this present life that confirm he is in control. So here is why I believe so strongly in an all powerful God who loves each one of us.

Stepping off Ledges

In a familiar movie scene, an explorer stands on a rocky ledge and stares across a deep gorge. Then he closes his eyes and steps forward, half expecting to plunge to his death far below. Instead, his foot lands safely on a stone bridge that has been remarkably camouflaged. The scene is from "Indiana Jones and the Last Crusade," and Jones is seeking the "Holy Grail" – the cup that Jesus used at the Last Supper. Along the way, the movie connects miracles with principles of Christian faith. The result is great entertainment.

Outside Hollywood, a walk of faith has a deeper purpose than mere entertainment. In real life, God's intervention is often desperately needed, and in one way the movie had it right. Sometimes seeing God work requires stepping off cliffs, and that is often the path we must take if we are to learn to trust God. So this is a book about the struggle for faith, stepping off cliffs, and little miracles.

Fortunately, most cliffs for us are not like the one in the movie, yet there are parallels. In the movie, Indiana could have played it safe if he had given up on his quest, but instead he embraced a higher goal than mere survival – one with eternal aspects. In fact, staying safe might have stifled the little faith he had already mustered, so he gambled his very life on the hope there was something more.

Testimonies are Important

This book relates personal experiences. In doing so it outlines a similar journey – a faith journey – with its many twists and turns. I offer it to you because scripture tells us that testimonies have power on a level that the book of Revelation compares to Christ's sacrifice on the cross. In Revelation 12 we read that those who follow Christ will ultimately overcome by "the blood of the lamb, and by the word of their testimony."

A testimony is a personal experience that goes deeper than just head knowledge or religion or moral values. Scripture reveals that testimonies are meant to be told. For example, Philemon 1:6 tells us "That the communication of your faith may become effective by the acknowledging of every good thing which is in you in Christ Jesus." So when we acknowledge what Christ has done in our lives, we make our faith "effective."

So one purpose of this book is to offer little gifts of faith to some of you who may be new to following Christ, since you may still be lacking faith experiences of your own. I was once in that condition. And also for those of you who are more experienced in your faith, it is hoped these stories will impart encouragement, for we can all use some of that.

8

I believe it can do this because I have continued to benefit personally from these experiences, and not just from these, but also from reading many other testimonies that others have shared.

Like many, if I am honest I tend to be a skeptic at heart. Sometimes doubt overcomes my faith, and that is why I need to remember times God has stepped in, and also why I feel motivated to write things down. Many other Christians have stories of God's provision, but if they are not recorded and told they are often lost and forgotten. That seems sad. The precedent that scripture sets is one of writing down records of God's miracles for future generations to read. So in its simplest form, this book is an attempt to do just that.

Some of the testimonies in this book are unusual – even extraordinary. It has been said that extraordinary claims require extraordinary evidence. For that reason, I have done my best to be as transparent as possible regarding names, places, and dates so that others may confirm these things are true. Another reason I have for including names is so when and if the named individuals read this book they will be able to identify with the experiences they participated in, which may then also become an encouragement to them.

When I was younger, testimonies like these helped me realize this faith thing is real. I am deeply grateful to those who have told what God has done. Some of these testimonies were from pastors, some were told by fellow Christians, some were found in scripture, and some were from other books. Besides the Bible, books that have strengthened my faith include *Hey God!*, by Frank Foglio, *God's Smuggler*, by Brother Andrew, *China Cry*, by Nora Lam, *The Cross and the Switchblade*, by David Wilkerson, and *"Journey on the Hard Side of Miracles,"* by Steven Stiles. In other words, past testimonies that tell how God has worked miracles have energized my own spiritual growth.

Testimonies are stories told by those who have experienced God. You see, with regards to any topic, I would rather trust the word of those who say they have experienced it, than to trust the word of those who have not. The first perspective comes from firsthand knowledge, while the other comes from a lack of the same.

Remembering the past can inspire the future. Seeing what God has done can increase expectations for what God is going to do. Brenda and I have certainly noticed our faith grow stronger as we have reminisced about the miracles, experiences, and coincidences in this book – ones that have defined our very personal life journeys.

Dare I say coincidences? The word is so often misunderstood. It simply refers to an unlikely alignment of events. I believe that such alignments, especially in answer to prayer, are from the hand of God. So I will continue to use the word sparingly, but please understand I don't take coincidences lightly. I am always talking about God's intervention, and I consider them to be little miracles. I believe God can use coincidences to show us he loves us, is with us, and can even point us to where he wants us to go.

So out of necessity this book is written from a first person perspective. That is a particularly challenging way to write, and I ask you to be somewhat forgiving as you read. I have tried hard to keep ego at bay, and I hope you can see that. If you end up thinking this is a book about the author, then I have failed. On the other hand, if you perceive this is a book about the Author of life, then it is a success.

Finally, a journey has many steps. A spiritual one can last a lifetime, and people of faith trust it will last for eternity. So now I offer for your consideration a journey of personal experiences that illustrate a few ways the master of the universe can participate in the lives of ordinary human beings.

* * *

CHAPTER 1

First Steps

A journey usually begins with a first step. Faith journeys are no different. In my case, that first step occurred when I was very young. There was a time my family lived in Bingen, Washington. It is located on the banks of the Columbia River across from Oregon and the snow-capped Mount Hood. On a cool day in January, 1957, a train pulled up to the depot. It was a scenario I would see on several occasions as I grew older. A train would pull up, and a conductor would grab the handrail and swing to the ground. He would then retrieve wood steps and place them next to the train car. On this day, he helped a young woman and two small boys into the arms of her waiting husband. At eighteen months of age, I was the smaller of the two boys.

Earlier, my parents had graduated from Northwestern Bible College in Minneapolis where they met. They then learned of a small group in Washington seeking a pastor. In response, as my father tells it, he booked a train ride west. The group then drafted a charter and chose the name, "Grace Baptist Church." Not long after, my mom, brother, and I also made the trip. Within days, we moved into a small house near the train tracks, between the local sawmill and the river.

Grace Baptist first met in a building on Bingen's main street, and some of my earliest memories include walking a short distance on warm Sunday evenings to services. Not long after, the church moved to a large house, also nearby. At those meetings, I recall annoying pats on the head, and playing in the back with my older brother Steve. During one evening service, we were too loud, and my mother pleaded

The railroad depot in Bingen, Washington as it appears today.

with us, promising ice cream if we behaved. The gimmick worked, and visits to an ice cream stand became a regular Sunday evening treat.

However, to us kids, the most important thing in our lives however, was not church – it was trains. Since trains ran past only a block away, we would watch them go by in amazement. Then, in 1959, Oregon observed their 100-year Centennial celebration of statehood. My grandparents visited from Wisconsin, and we attended. To a four-year old it was amazing. Steve and I were in awe when we rode a tour train around the grounds, and for months afterward, our little red wagon became that train. We would pull it around our yard so often that we wore a lasso-shaped trail into the lawn – to the frustration of our parents.

It was as we pulled the wagon around that path that I recall my first discussion about faith. You see, in those days, Steve and I did not think faith was complicated. But on this day, as we pulled the wagon we strongly disagreed about a memory. After much arguing we finally agreed that someday in heaven we would learn who was right.

We also believed that God could do anything. At some point, our parents led us in a simple prayer to ask Jesus to come into our hearts. For more than a decade, that prayer was the depth of my relationship with God. But even

12

today I look back at those experiences as important first steps in a spiritual journey.

One futuristic small scale train at the 1959 Oregon Centennial celebration.

When I was five, the church moved up the side of the mountain to the town of White Salmon. Our family followed, moving into a house on Spring Street. Services were held in the Grange Hall, also known as the Odd Fellows Hall. I can't believe I still remember those names. On Sunday mornings we attended Sunday School, where we learned Bible stories and songs including, "Jesus Loves Me," and "Jesus Loves the Little Children." After morning services, my brother and I would approach the pianist and ask for candy, and she would invariably dig a couple of Hershey's kisses out of her purse. We thought it was wonderful, until one day Mom suggested that begging for candy was rude. After that, we no longer asked.

Early Memories

Winters in White Salmon were mild compared to the Midwest where I now live, but it would still snow. One blizzard dumped so much that I couldn't see over the edges

Grace Baptist Church moved from Bingen to White Salmon, Washington, into this Grange Hall building, also known as the Odd Fellows Hall. Here it is seen in a street view photo from Google Maps. In 1960 it was painted white, and had a gravel parking lot.

of the shoveled walks – an experience I thought was incredible. But the snow could also make driving on mountain roads treacherous. My dad would put chains on the tires, which is a practice I have not seen since, since the Midwest is so flat.

One of the roads that was most treacherous ran up the side of the mountain overlooking a lagoon. Steve and I were afraid of it, and would beg our parents to not drive on it. But it was often the shortest way home, so we often lost that battle, and I was still too young to understand the concept of placing things into God's hands.

In 1961 we moved to Washington Street, and our house faced south. Through the front window we had a great view of the snow-capped Mount Hood across the river, a view that my brother and I simply took for granted.

When I started first grade we would walk a few blocks to a modern, single story brick school. My teacher's name was Mrs. Logan, and I recall her insistence that we cut smooth curves with scissors, and her frustration – not to mention mine – that I seemed unable to grasp the meaning of words on paper.

Eventually her efforts paid off, and sentences like "see spot run" came alive. Then, before second grade, my dad accepted a position as an associate pastor at Harbor Baptist Church in Hoquaim, Washington, a city southwest of Seattle and close to the Pacific shoreline, and we moved.

All of this may not seem to have much to do with a spiritual journey, but journey's often begin small. Soon little miracles would come that would dramatically shape my young faith.

* * *

*

CHAPTER 2

God Protects us in the Storm

Second grade for me began in Hoquaim, Washington. By this time Steve and I had two younger siblings, Karen and Keith. One Friday evening after dark, the chore of washing dishes was mine. As I toiled over the sink, a glance out the window revealed trees and bushes whipping wildly in the wind. When I ran to the living room to tell my mom, she said I should stop imagining things and go back to washing dishes. Just as I began to protest, the lights went out. Thankfully, the dishes were forgotten.

The next few hours were frightening as high winds buffeted the house. Our dad was across town at a church board meeting, and our mom took charge by leading us in a prayer for safety. Then the five of us huddled by candlelight on the living room couch, watching a large picture window bow dangerously inward only a few feet in front of us. Fortunately, with our prayers and God's grace the window held.

By sunrise the wind subsided. It was only then that my mom realized how much danger we were in from the bowing window. In fact, with all the noise from the wind we didn't realize that an upstairs window directly above the picture window actually broke during the storm. Mom regretted not moving us away from the window, but expressed thankfulness that God protected us. Was it a miracle? I wasn't sure, but for me this became my first awareness that God can answer prayer, and mainly because my mom gathered us to pray.

Soon my dad made it home, and told of power lines and trees down everywhere. In addition to our upstairs broken window, he found that our chimney had also fallen over. Many trees on our street, including our neighbor's, were also uprooted. And then, of great interest to my brother and I, a two-story house about a block west of ours became a single story house when its lower level collapsed.

The storm was originally called Typhoon Freda, but it struck on Columbus Day in October, 1962, and came to be known as the Columbus Day storm. Thanks to the modern wonder of the Internet, I have learned that it has been called "the most powerful windstorm to strike the Pacific Northwest in the 20th Century." (Wolf Read, Phd., 2018).

Pennies from Heaven

And this storm was just the first of two faith lessons that month. Not many days later the Cuban Missile Crisis also required prayer. One Friday afternoon teachers at our school announced we might soon find Russia had conquered America, and communist soldiers had replaced all our teachers.

To a seven-year-old this seemed really bad, so it was time for action. The Sunday morning service motivated me to put my new-found faith to work, so I asked God to send money to buy weapons to defend the United States. And I even set a time limit. I made it clear that I expected an answer by bedtime!

By the end of the Sunday evening service my prayer hadn't been answered. But then a small miracle happened. As I was walking toward the door, a younger kid asked me if I would like some money! I knew this was the answer to my prayer, and I said "Yes!" But then he only placed eight cents in my hand.

I knew eight cents wouldn't buy tanks, but even though it didn't seem like much, I think my inability to explain away this simple answer to prayer helped keep me from the brink of spiritual idiocy as a teen when I was tempted to buy into the faithless view that God isn't real, or

A scene from Newberg, Oregon after the Columbus Day storm of October 12, 1962.

that prayer is powerless.

Second grade was also the year that Sunday School lessons began sinking in. Basic life choices became front and center, such as whether to live selfishly, or to live for God and others. The temptation was to simply toss out faith and lie, cheat, and steal, or do whatever advances one's own cause. Of course the other option was to treat others as you would wish to be treated.

In the end, the Golden Rule was persuasive. I decided that Christ's command to "Do unto others as you would have others do unto you" contained simple logic that is hard to deny. I suspect the paths of many other lives have been altered – and improved – by those few words. As years passed I became aware that many have rejected the Golden Rule altogether and chosen to live lives filled with selfish ambition, arguments, fighting, rants and discord. So I am glad for those early Sunday School lessons.

A 1962 photo of the Hatch family standing in front of Harbor Baptist Church in Aberdeen, Washington. Shown are my parents, Duane and Lois, along with us kids. From left to right are seen Keith in Dad's arms, Karen, myself smirking, and Steve. My mom passed away in 1985, and my dad remarried Vanie (not shown), who is therefore my step-mom. My dad is still active in his 90s.

* * *

CHAPTER 3

Grandfathers' Angels

When I was in third grade, we moved to Wisconsin to share a home for a few months with my mom's parents – my grandparents. My grandfather, John Longard, didn't talk a lot. When he did it always seemed to be with wit and wisdom. It was then he told a story that had lasting impact on me.

The story took place in the fall of 1947. He purchased a motorcycle and managed to run it off the road into a ditch not far from home. The result was a broken back, and other injuries. He then found himself floating up and away from his lifeless body. He watched as an ambulance crew arrived and loaded his body onto a stretcher. And then he was met by an angel who took his hand and asked if he was ready to die. He thought about how his family depended on him, and replied in the negative. Then suddenly he found himself back in his body in great pain, in the ambulance. Later on, the doctor told him he was lucky to be alive, since the accident had seriously bruised his spinal chord.

I found this story to be memorable, and assumed it was a rare experience. It also seemed to be strong evidence that angels and Heaven were real. Not long after hearing this story, we moved to Illinois. A few years passed, and then I heard a similar story from my other grandfather.

He told the story after I turned twelve. We drove from Illinois to Phoenix to visit my dad's parents. Richard Hatch had spent a lifetime farming, but now was semi-retired. Unfortunately, he was suffering from emphysema, and his doctor said it resulted from farming dust since he had never smoked.

He told how one night he was having great difficulty breathing, and was in torment. Suddenly, he found himself floating above his body in the darkness of his bedroom, and he was totally free of pain. He was amused that even though the room was pitch black, he could still see his body as clearly as in the light of day. Then he floated up and away through the ceiling into a long dark tunnel toward a bright light in the distance. Along the way, he was met by an angel who asked if he was ready to die. Like my other grandfather, after thinking of his family, he said he was not ready. Then, also like my other grandfather, he found himself back in his body, again in pain and struggling to breathe.

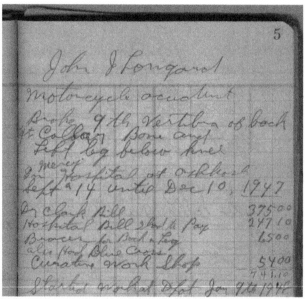

A page from my grandfather Longard's journal describing details and medical costs of his motorcycle accident.

For me at the time, it seemed my grandfather's stories proved that the supernatural realm was real. Years later, when the book "Life after Life" was published, everyone else became aware such experiences were actually common. But for me, when I went through a faith crisis as a teenager, my grandfather's stories helped me to not discard my faith.

* * *

*

CHAPTER 4

WWII Promise

Around this time, my dad, Duane Hatch, told us kids a story about a promise God gave him. As World War II raged on, he turned 18 and was sure he would be drafted. Since he was determined to never kill any person, he decided to apply as a conscientious objector. But after praying about it, he believed God gave him a promise that if he enlisted he would never see fighting. And so it was that he decided to enlist in the US army on the basis of a God-given promise.

As an enlisted man, the Army sent him to Yale University for six months of training. After six months, the war was over, and the Army then sent him to Japan to inspect factories for weapon making activities. And so it was that he never had to fight, and God's promise to him was fulfilled.

I always found this story to be inspiring, and then, as I entered my teenage years, God also gave me a similar promise, but for a different war.

Vietnam Promise

In 1970, the United States was fighting in Vietnam. Men were being drafted into the Army at a record pace, and many were returning home in body bags. So, in order to be more equitable about who would be drafted, the United States began a lottery system. Birth dates were drawn at random and assigned numbers based on the order they were drawn. The lower your number, the more likely you would be drafted.

When the lottery began, I was only fourteen and too young to be drafted. But I knew the lottery for my birth year would come in a few years, and I was worried. So on the day of the very first lottery I asked God if he would grant me a sign as to whether I would be drafted, even though this wasn't the lottery that would determine my fate.

In the request, I was very specific. I asked that if God would promise me that I would not be drafted, then he would have my birthday – June 8th – drawn as the very last one. It seemed like a big request, but I wanted to believe that God could do that, and that he might. So when the lottery drawing was to begin, I sat in our driveway listening to the car radio. I then paid close attention as every date was drawn, beginning with number one. They were painfully slow, and it went on for quite awhile, but my attention never drifted. Finally, they drew number 364, and my birthday had not been drawn! I was rather excited as it seemed God had answered my prayer – my birthday was to be number 365! But when they pulled number 365, it wasn't my birthday, and I felt dread and disbelief. I wondered how I could have missed hearing it. But then, just as I was about to turn off the radio, they announced one more date would be drawn. It was number 366! I had forgotten that leap years have 366 days, and February 29th had also been a date in the lottery. So the very last number drawn was June 8th - my birthday! They gave it the number 366, and I claimed it as a promise from God that I would not be drafted.

A few years later, when the lottery for my birth year arrived, the number that was drawn for my birthday was low enough that it seemed I might be drafted. I admit I was worried, but I wanted to believe that God would fulfill his promise. However, a few months later it was announced that we would withdraw from the Vietnam war completely. As a result, I never received a draft notice, and God proved his promise to me to be true.

* * *

CHAPTER 5

Amazing Testimonies

In spite of these answers to prayer and my grandfather's stories, during my teen years I still struggled with whether or not God is real. I also slipped into a state of depression. But change was coming. One day, a man named Brian Ruud spoke at a student assembly in our high school gym. Brian had electric enthusiasm and a blond afro as big as a volley ball. In his testimony, he told how a life of crime and drugs put him in prison. This then led him to a turning point where he surrendered to a higher power. Finally, he told how the court system released him when fingerprints on a bottle he knew he had handled no longer matched his actual fingerprints. It was the only real evidence the system had against him, so now they had to release him. Brian concluded that God miraculously changed his fingerprints!

Ruud's testimony was inspirational and my brother and I told our parents about it. They then took us to see him at First Assembly in Rockford, where Pastor Whitcomb had invited him to speak. There we heard his story again, in greater detail. And here he openly gave credit to Jesus for saving him, without holding back.

Then, not long after, I was exiting my high school when a youth stopped me. He said he was from "The House of Bread," based in some nearby church. He said to me, "Jesus Christ changed my life," and he told me that he could do the same for me. Before we parted, he gave me a copy of "The Cross and the Switchblade," by David Wilkerson. I read the book straight through, and learned how Wilkerson made a radical decision to leave comfort behind in Pennsylvania and move to New York to work with street gangs. It was a decision based on only a Life magazine photo and article,

Brian Ruud, as he appears on the cover of one of his books.

and the sense that God was calling him to get involved. I was particularly impressed with how Wilkerson made decisions after praying for and receiving guidance from God. He seemed to experience miraculous outcomes from such decisions, and I knew that I desired such a relationship with God, but didn't know how to get it.

Turning Point

For Christmas in my senior year, my parents gave me a copy of the Living New Testament. As I read it, I was drawn to a growing sense that the early Christians lived lives rooted in love for God and each other. At the same time, I recall realizing that I was bankrupt in both areas.

A turning point came in Physics class when I refused to let anyone help me thread tape through an expensive video recorder, and thus damaged fragile wire pickups inside the head. This caused both teachers and peers to ostracize me, creating an emotional crisis. A night or two later, in the quiet of my room, I prayed a prayer that went something like this:

"Jesus, I'm in a mess and I don't even know if you're real. I guess I never decided to follow you – at least not like the New Testament Christians. I guess if you're not real, I have nothing to lose. So here's the deal. If you can figure out how to show me what you want me to do, I'll do it, no matter what."

In that instant something changed. I am not really sure what, but suddenly the fog of depression lifted, and I felt an amazing sense of being loved. Then I drifted off to sleep. The next morning I woke up feeling great. This was incredibly unusual, and I tried to figure out why. I recall thinking, "It's not my birthday, and it's not Christmas!" It was only then that I remembered my deal from the night before.

At this point, I began to read the Bible in earnest, discovering it took on a whole new dimension. Instead of just seeing it as ancient history, it was as though God was speaking to me personally and challenging my lack of faith and love. I had been actually loving no one, and Jesus was commanding me to love *everyone,* even my enemies, with no exceptions. It had an effect. After about two days my sister asked why I was not fighting with her anymore. When I told her about my experience she said, "Well whatever happened to you, I like it!"

So I found that surrendering to Jesus broke a cycle of depression. Before this, I had spent months striving on my own to break free from depression and find purpose in life. But all my best efforts had backfired, while simply surrendering to God did not.

* * *

*

CHAPTER 6

God Fixes a Bad Decision

As high school graduation neared, a couple of local companies handed out job applications. I filled them out, and by graduation was able to choose between two jobs. The first company offered two years of engineering school while allowing me to work half-days as a machinist in a clean comfortable environment. The second company wanted to put me on a machine making cutting tools in a dirty shop without air-conditioning, and with no educational bonus. But I was naive.

In my youthful idealism I did not listen to my parents, and therefore did not make the obviously wise choice. Instead, I accepted the second option, and began working in less than ideal circumstances. My reasoning was that I had decided to go to Bible college, and I did not feel I would work at the better factory long enough to repay them for the free education!

I quickly regretted turning down the better offer, as I spent my days working in sweltering temperatures with sub-standard training. So I promised God that if the other company called again and asked me to reconsider, I would consider that a sign, and would go to work for them. But honestly, it seemed that the chance of this happening was next to nothing, and I really thought I had made a terrible mistake.

I am so thankful that sometimes God intervenes when we make dumb decisions. After two weeks, the first company called back and indeed did ask if I would reconsider. I believed this to be a miracle, and so it was that I quit my first job and began a job at Woodward Governor Company, where I would ultimately gain two years of engineering education, and ten years of work experience.

Coincidental Invitations

Not long after I entered the engineering program, Gary, one of my fellow students invited me to a youth Bible Study. That evening, as I was getting ready, there was another little miracle. My sister was also getting ready to go somewhere, and it turned out she was also invited to this same Bible study! So Karen and I rode together, along with her friend Laura who invited her.

That night, there were about fifteen youth in attendance, and some at the Bible study placed their hands on Karen's head and shoulders and began praying for her to receive the Baptism in the Holy Spirit. Suddenly, she began sobbing, and then laughing and speaking rapidly in what sounded like another language. This was quite uncharacteristic for her. For both of us it was our first experience with the phenomenon of the Biblical gift of speaking in tongues, and we had happened onto a service similar to the one in Acts chapter eight where people were praying to receive it.

This then began a period where I actively sought to also speak in tongues, for I wanted what Karen had, and rationalized that I wanted all that God could offer. But after weeks of intensely seeking the experience, nothing had happened.

Months passed, and then finally one evening after a particularly inspiring youth meeting I was worshiping God in private. And then it happened. Suddenly, my tongue began moving rapidly in what was clearly another language. I was amazed at the precise rhythms and sounds, and then as quickly as it started it stopped. It was as though, to my dismay, my mind regained control of my tongue. But I was left with a deep sense that God loved me enough to let me experience this, and that speaking in tongues could be a genuine spiritual experience.

Over the years, however, I have tried on occasion to experience this gift again without success. During the following decades I have belonged to churches of various denominations, and have come to the conviction that the experience can be both beneficial and divisive – a perspective that is Biblical. I believe the beneficial aspects are primarily that it increases the faith of the one who experiences it. But biblically speaking, it is one of the least gifts, simply because it has little value for others unless they happen to speak that language, like those in the book of Acts. The workaround that Paul gives us is that when tongues are spoken in public they should also be publicly interpreted. But it is then the interpretation that has the greater value.

For me, the bottom line is that sensitivity to the Holy Spirit is needed when exercising any spiritual gift in any setting. That sensitivity is sometimes lacking. On the other hand, I have met many Christians who have never spoken in tongues, yet clearly have experienced God's amazing presence in their lives, and are excited about their relationship with Jesus. For these reasons, I have found that I feel at home in any church that honors Christ passionately, without regard to whether or not they encourage the gift of tongues publicly. The bottom line is that I believe in God's eyes your denomination is not what matters, but rather it is your relationship with Jesus.

My Sister Healed

About this time, a healing evangelist named Roxanne Brant held a week of services at First Assembly in Rockford. My sister Karen and I attended, along with others from our youth group. Roxanne did not fit the stereotype of a "faith healer", for she had a gracious and quiet personality. In her

A low resolution photo of Roxanne Brant as she appeared in the 1970s.

services, she led people into the presence of God to a degree that I had not experienced in church services prior to that.

Karen was praying for healing from back pain after a classmate pulled a chair out from under her as she sat down. A vertebrate in her back had been dislodged, and it took frequent trips to the chiropractor to put it back into place. However, during one service, Roxanne looked directly at Karen and told her that her back was being healed. Karen says that her back then became hot, and after that she no longer suffered pain. When the chiropractor called she went in to see him. He said that the vertebrate was still in place, and she told him that God had healed her. He replied that he gets that a lot.

At the time, Roxanne Brant seemed controversial. She said that God showed her the future, and that the Watergate scandal, which had just surfaced in the news, would become a major event for America. She also foretold a recession, and predicted earthquakes would become more common in the United States. For Florida, she said that flooding would become a problem for one-fifth of the state, which caused her to change her plans and buy land in Jacksonville, which had a higher elevation. She also warned of major power outages, and said she saw the word "Storm" in big letters. Then she claimed that in the future, store shelves would be lined with herbal supplements which God had created for our health. It was this last claim that actually caused me the most doubt, partly because I had no belief that herbs could be beneficial. But other things also troubled me. She insisted that earth's poles would begin to melt, even though scientists were telling us we were entering another ice age. Global warming was not even a concept in those days. The bottom line? It seems that everything I can recall her saying has already happened, or is coming to pass.

* * *

*

CHAPTER 7

Voted Out

The youth meetings that my sister and I attended were held in a nice exposed lower level of a Lutheran Church. The meetings were led by church members Chuck and Sharon Mueller who had a gift for relating to teens. An adult group was also meeting at the same church under the leadership of the senior pastor. Both groups were growing, and a number of people today can trace spiritual roots back to these simple meetings.

But, there were those in the church who were uneasy with the fact that some people meeting there were not members, and they were also concerned about reports of miracles, healings, and speaking in tongues. So the church convened a special meeting to vote on whether they would continue to allow this to continue. We were all invited. After much debate, a vote was taken. The result was that we were asked to leave, as was the church's pastor, Walter Lamp.

When the adults left, they started a new non-denominational church, and named it Church of the Living Water. Walter Lamp became their pastor, and I attended there for awhile, as did my father. We enjoyed their quiet spirit and miracle working faith, and I also came to see similar qualities in my dad. These were people who prayed for the impossible and often saw it happen. One elderly couple would come almost every week with amazing testimonies of doors that God had opened for them to minister to others, and of miracles that God had done for them that week. On one memorable occasion, I recall that a blind women who lived in the neighborhood asked for prayer. When people prayed for her, she became very excited and claimed she was able to see.

Galilee House

When the youth group left the church, we had nowhere to go. We had taken the Lutheran church's facilities for granted, and the Church of the Living Water, while fine for Sunday services, was not the youth's idea of a great place to hang out. For a while we met in Chuck and Sharon's living room, and prayed about what to do next. It was the mid '70s, and it seemed every town in America had a Christian coffeehouse. So Chuck and Sharon talked to friends, raised donations, and soon we opened our own coffeehouse. It was located in two storefronts on the southwest corner of Kishwaukee and 15th Avenue in Rockford. We painted the name Galilee House on the windows, and prepared to host singers and bands for events on Friday and Saturday evenings. I helped strip the floors of tile and lay down natural wood planks for flooring. I also participated in making tables from Electric company cable spools, and helped fabricate, stain, and varnish a plywood food bar. Future Congressman Don Manzullo managed to gain us non-profit status, and before long we were open for business.

Soon, Christian artists were coming from all around to entertain in front of multi-colored floodlights. We served free popcorn and soda pop was also available. The result was that often the place was packed.

* * *

CHAPTER 8

Premonition or Protection?

Around this time, I moved out of my parents home into an apartment with four other roommates. We called our household "The Holy Ghost Workshop," which we also used as a greeting for answering the phone. One day, I was driving my car north along North Second Street in Rockford and exited onto Forest Hills Road. Suddenly I had a premonition in which I saw a newspaper headline saying "Rockford Man Dies in Crash." I somehow knew that this headline was about my own death, which I also knew was about to occur at the intersection of Forest Hills and River Lane about a mile ahead.

I had never experienced a premonition before, and was pretty sure this was just an overactive imagination. Still, I decided to be ready to brake just in case I was wrong. As I approached the intersection, I saw a car parked on the right shoulder, and two men leaning against the fender. Nothing at all seemed dangerous about the situation. But then, to my surprise, a white car I had not seen behind the other car backed out of the ditch directly across my path. I locked up the brakes and was barely able to avoid a collision. Without the premonition, I believe I would have hit it. The experience was quite unique, and in all the years since, I have never experienced anything quite like it.

While some would attribute such an experience to some mystical psychic force, I believe that such an interpretation makes no sense because only an omniscient being could know what was about to transpire and come up with a plan to change the outcome. In other words, the only logical explanation is that the premonition was from God. Furthermore, this is one of several experiences that have convinced me, in addition to the Bible, that God knows the future, and that he cares about our well-being. Sometimes, when difficult times come my way, I think about experiences like this, and it seems easier to trust that "all things work together for good for those who love the Lord." (Romans 8:28).

Sometimes I think that the reason people are quick to credit a "sixth sense" or "the universe" with being the source of good things is because to give God credit would also mean we might be expected to walk in God's ways. Yet I am convinced God's ways not only make the most sense, but they are also the most fulfilling way to live life. As the prophet Hosea noted,

> "Who is wise? He will realize these things. Who is discerning? He will understand them. The ways of the LORD are right; the righteous walk in them, but the rebellious stumble in them." Hosea 14:8-9 NIV

Street Witnessing

During one evening at Galilee House Coffeehouse, I felt that God was calling me to witness more boldly for Christ. Now you need to understand, that by nature I tend to be introverted, and especially at that age I experienced daily panic attacks in social situations. Still, as you may also recall, a similar encounter had been significant for me when a youth stopped me and gave me his testimony. So now, I began contemplating big change. I think it would be accurate to say that in those days, I was intent on finding the will of God almost to a fault, if that is possible.

So on this evening, I told God that if no-one invited me to go street witnessing with them that very same evening, I would take that as a sign, and would move to Chicago to join Jesus People USA. JPUSA was a Christian community that practiced street witnessing. It should be noted that I had never been invited to go witnessing before, nor was I aware of anyone doing this in Rockford, so it seemed like I had already made the decision to move.

As the night wore on, I prayed fervently, because I really did not want to move to Chicago, and I am honestly not sure if I would have followed through with that commitment. When the music ended, the audience went home. Still, no one approached me. So I hung around and cleaned tables, than sat down and read my Bible. Finally, close to the time of locking the doors, Chuck Mueller approached and asked if I would be willing to organize a group of volunteers to do street ministry in Rockford! I accepted his offer in a most embarrassing fashion, with tears and emotion. He also said I was not the first person he asked, but others had turned him down. He may have been taken aback by my emotional response, but Chuck and Sharon published a brief account of God's answer to my prayer in that month's newsletter. I still have the Galilee House newsletter that mentions that conversation – a conversation that became another step in my spiritual journey.

During the next two years, I would lead a small group of youth out into the streets of Rockford as we did our best to tell people about Christ. And during those outings, several people prayed to receive Christ, while others asked us to pray with them for other things. We also led several people with serious addictions or problems to enter Teen Challenge or JPUSA.

Yet in spite of some success, I felt this was a difficult calling. To approach strangers when one has not been invited and to communicate the gospel with love was daunting. I could tell this was not what I was gifted at, although others who went out with us did seem somewhat more suited for the task. Whenever we went out, rejection was common, and each time I would dread going out. In the end, however, the net result seemed beneficial for the Kingdom of God, and was certainly beneficial for my own spiritual growth.

A Dream about JPUSA

Around this time, I experienced a dream that involved my sister Karen. At the time of the dream, my sister was sharing a room with her friend Laura, who became interested in moving to JPUSA. Karen had mentioned to me that she was giving Laura a ride to visit them on an upcoming weekend, but I had totally forgotten this fact by the time the weekend rolled around.

On Saturday afternoon I took a nap. During the nap, I dreamed that Karen had moved to JPUSA, and that I had come to visit. As I pulled up in front of the building, Karen walked out. I noticed that she seemed unusually happy. Then I woke up to find myself repeating aloud the words, "Karen is moving to Jesus People. Karen is moving to Jesus People."

About the time I realized what I was saying, the phone rang, and I picked up. It was Karen. She asked, "Guess what?" Without even thinking I replied, "You're moving to Jesus People!" She let out a squeal and begged, "How could you possibly know that?" I told her about the dream I had just had. Then she told me that she had prayed with counselors at the ministry, and had agreed with them that if God gave her a sign, she would move there. So, she considered my dream the sign she was looking for, and she did indeed move in with them for three months. She later told me that the dream was fulfilled, for during those months she was unusually happy. Later she left, partly because she missed her boyfriend and future husband. But she always considered those three months in Chicago a special time of spiritual growth.

Protected in a Car Crash

Not long after the previous dream, I also had another dream. I had purchased a brand new Renault LeCar and had only driven it less than a year before I slid off the left side of a road in a blizzard and struck a tree. The accident was severe, and in fact, the car was virtually demolished.

The passenger side of the car struck the tree. When it came to rest, the tree was only an inch from the steering wheel. I was thankful that no one was riding with me, for the passenger would have been crushed. Afterward, the police officer insisted on calling an ambulance, given the severity of the crash. But I believe God had protected me. At the hospital they found that only about one square inch of my scalp looked as though it had been shaved with a razor. Otherwise, except for aches and pains, the ER staff could find nothing wrong.

And then, later that night I dreamed I was driving the same car on the same road I had crashed on. Up ahead I saw the back of a man walking away from me on the same side of the road where I crashed. He had long hair, was wearing what looked like a white bathrobe, and I thought, "Why would anyone wear a bathrobe in public, out in the middle of nowhere." So I began to wonder who he might be. At first I thought he was homeless, but as I got closer I could see that the robe looked too nice, so I thought he must be a monk from some nearby monastery.

Then, as I came up behind him he turned around and looked directly at me. Instead of the face of a homeless or religious person, I was startled to see a face that radiated love, and I was struck by the conviction that this person cared about my well-being. I then woke up. It was only then, when I was fully awake, that I realized that this person walking along the side of the road must have been Jesus! To me, the significance of the dream was that Jesus was letting me know that he had protected me during the car crash. The simple fact that I did not recognize him until after I woke up and processed the clues convinced me that my brain had not concocted this dream, but rather it was from God.

* * *

CHAPTER 9

Apartment Makeover

In the late 1970s, I played a flute-like instrument known as a recorder, and was in a music group known as "Bread of Life." We played in various venues around the area. But I was still single. It was before I met Brenda, and I was feeling depressed and lonely.

I prayed for a solution, and mentioned my condition to Cindy, my downstairs neighbor – a gal who was a Christian, married, and a singer in our music group. Cindy suggested that I begin by giving my messy apartment a makeover. I accepted the challenge, and immediately devoted myself to cleaning, decorating, and putting up curtains. In fact, I even used my newfound determination to make a variety of artwork by decoupaging magazine pictures on pieces of scrap wood, and hanging them on the walls. Then, with the addition of a few scented candles I found that the apartment indeed became a more soothing and relaxing place, and my depression lifted.

Girls

I then allowed a Christian roommate to move in. Joe was also single, and he was the piano player in our group. One night, Joe was away at a church function, and I was feeling particularly lonely. So I prayed for a solution. God spoke to me through a scripture which said simply, "Let them marry whom they think best." To me, this simple line of scripture suggested that I should find a girl of my choosing and marry her. The advice was so simple and obvious that I found it to be stunning.

An hour or so later, my roommate arrived home and told me that he had met a girl that he was falling in love with, but he wanted a sign from God to know if he should ask her to marry him. I shared with him the verse that I had just found, and he claimed it as the sign he was looking for. A few months later I attended their wedding. Meanwhile, my own search had been activated.

At the Overflowing Cup Christian Coffeehouse in Beloit, Wisconsin, I paid closer attention to the girls than I had in the past. And then, there she was. I thought I found the girl that seemed to be the perfect one for me. Instead of being pretentious like so many others, she seemed so down to earth that it took my breath away. Her name was Brenda, and I asked her out.

Afterwards, as I stood on the front steps of the building, I realized that the date was 8/8/78, a date that we still celebrate as an anniversary. Biblically, I had always associated the number eight with new beginnings, and this date did indeed become a new beginning for both of us. It took us longer than my roommate, but two and one-half years later we were married. Sometimes I like to refer to Brenda as my first wife or my last wife, but both are true for we are still married. And no, you don't have to worry, I'm not quitting my day job!

Buried in snow

The winter of '78 and '79 was brutal. One day there was a terrible blizzard. After spending time together, I dropped Brenda off at her parents' house in the country. Conditions were worsening rapidly as I headed for home. After going about a mile, I was blinded by blowing snow, and the car veered into a tall snow drift that was partly blocking the road. Now I was stuck, and could go nowhere.

With no other options, I began the long walk back to Brenda's. But with a light windbreaker, I was not dressed for the weather. As I neared her house, I was cold and dizzy, and beginning to wonder if I would make it. I still recall struggling with great effort to manage the last fifty yards or so.

Once inside, my future father-in-law sprang into action. We hopped into his flatbed truck and headed for the car. by the time we arrived, the snow drift had completely covered it to the point that even the shape of the car was hidden. Only one corner of the rear bumper was still visible. Even the large truck was not able to easily pull the car out from under all that snow. It was only by jerking repeatedly on the chain that we managed to yank it out inch by inch.

In retrospect, I see the events of that day as signs that God protected me in another dangerous situation. If I had driven farther before encountering the whiteout, I might not have made it back to the house. If we had delayed any longer, we would not have been able to find the car beneath all the snow. And if it had stayed in that drift, the car would probably have been badly damaged when the plows finally came through. As it was, I was stranded for three days at the home of a girl I had fallen for, and I also missed work. In other words, the situation was not that bad!

The Music Group

Brenda and I continued to date, and around this time, a Bible study group that we were part of decided to begin singing in nursing homes. In an attempt to get it started right, I drafted several pages of rules that I thought would help. Then, as I left the house to go to practice, a special guest came on the FM radio station to discuss how to start a music ministry group. He argued that when starting a music group to minister one should not worry about being too professional. He specifically argued against leaders drafting up long lists of rules. By the time he was done I had thrown out the pages in hand and proceeded to go to practice and tell my story of what happened. We went on to sing in a number of nursing homes over the next year or so, all without the benefit of a list of rules. I still have a tape of one of our practice sessions, and it's really not that bad!

Bible School

During these years, I was attending First Assembly of God church, in Rockford, Illinois. First Assembly's founding pastor was Eugene Whitcomb. Pastor Whitcomb had died on September 11, 1974, when his small plane crashed on a mission trip to an Indian reservation. Besides being an enthusiastic pastor with a great preaching style, he was also the pastor who invited Brian Ruud and Roxanne Brant to speak – both of whom had an impact on my faith. I felt devastated by his death.

Pastor Whitcomb also seriously connected with youth in our city who had been alienated by religion in general. These were the years when the Jesus Revolution was winding down, and in those days the front of our large sanctuary was lined with hippie-styled long-haired youth. Many were in worn-out blue jeans, with some going barefoot or wearing sandals or halter tops – and he welcomed them all with enthusiasm.

When Pastor Whitcomb died in the plane crash, Ernie Moen, his former college roommate came for the funeral. He quickly won the hearts of the members with his sincere and simple style, and soon was asked to be the next pastor at First Assembly.

Pastor Moen connected with Rockford in uniquely different ways than Pastor Whitcomb. Now, instead of radical youth lining the front, he would play a movie or host a special speaker and fill the church with visitors. Then he would give altar calls where often as many as 200 people in one service would line the altar for salvation. I had never seen such services before, and yet it happened on a number of occasions. Even Pastor Moen said tearfully that he had never seen God move like that before. Today, we often cross paths with people who dedicated their lives to Christ during those services.

After I began dating Brenda, I was attending a Sunday evening service at church, and it was Pastor Moen who was preaching. During this service, I distinctly felt that God was telling me I needed to prepare for some type of ministry. This caused me to begin to earnestly seek answers from God by reading the Word and praying hard. I recall asking him if he wanted me to be a pastor, and I heard a clear answer, "Not exactly." With that re-direction, I began praying about the possibility of going to school with the goal of entering full time ministry. And it seemed God was beating around the bush, and by the time I had prayed through, I heard him essentially say, "You are going to be a late bloomer." I remember thinking, "What does this mean? Will I be really old, like 40, before I find a ministry?" This caused me some anxiety at first, and I wanted to know more, so I began to pray even more earnestly during the course of the next week.

The following Saturday we played mini-putt golf with friends, but I felt very distracted by a feeling that my future was hanging in the balance. I don't say this as an excuse, for I have no memory of how I scored. All I know is I wanted God to somehow give me a clue what the next step in my future should be, and that is all I could think about.

The next day was Sunday. As God would arrange it, Pastor Moen talked extensively about Christian Life School of the Bible. It was the Bible college that the church was operating, and I thought that I might sign up for it. Then he gave an altar call that I have never seen done before or since. He asked for anyone feeling that God might be calling them to go into full time ministry to come to the altar and receive prayer. To me, this was obviously the sign I was seeking, so I jumped up and practically sprinted to the front.

As a result of this commitment, I signed up for Bible school, and attended classes for the next three years. During that time I earned about one years worth of credit equivalents, which eventually were recognized in part when I attended Cardinal Stritch. But this was just another step in an educational journey, that would eventually span decades.

* * *

CHAPTER 10

Stranded

Not everything I learned during these years came from classes. God also had some life lessons to teach me. One of these lessons was to begin trusting God more. Putting things in God's hands can seem complicated. I suspect that when you lose yourself in worry to the point that you begin to beg God to eliminate the source of a worry, then too much praying can actually be a bad thing! This lesson became real to me on a Saturday in the summer of 1979 when Brenda and I were dating. I had picked her up earlier in the day, and now we rode my motorcycle north, to take her home. It was about twenty five miles each way, over country roads.

The bike was generally reliable, but on this day the plugs were fouling, the engine was sputtering, and it was barely able to go 25 mph. We started to worry that we wouldn't make it.

So I prayed fervently that the engine would keep running. In fact, I thought that the more I begged God, the more likely it would be that he would intervene. That actually does sound Biblical, doesn't it? But as mile after mile rolled by the bike was still barely running, and I felt less and less at peace because God wasn't intervening.

And then, suddenly my fears were realized. There was a loud noise and the bike wouldn't go any farther. "Aha!" I said. "the engine is finally shot." But as I got off the bike it became obvious that the engine was not the problem. Instead, the chain had derailed. This was something I had not experienced before, and it was not even remotely related to the plugs fouling. Without tools, I knew that I wouldn't be able to fix it, and here we were, stranded in a remote area about two miles from the nearest town.

This new situation was even more worrisome than the sputtering engine. And it was then that a little miracle occurred. The very first vehicle to come along was another motorcycle driven by a coworker of mine who worked with me in my department at the Woodward Governor Company, about fifteen miles south. He offered to give Brenda a ride on his bike to a phone. We were reluctant to accept his offer, because he was obviously drunk. But we didn't have any other options. So Brenda rode into town on the back of his bike, giving us both another worry to pray about. He then took her to a bar where Brenda recalls feeling intimidated, but she was able to call for help.

Later, with a new chain and new plugs, the bike was good for many more miles. I also realized that because the chain derailed exactly where and when it did, we weren't stranded for long. In other words, God came through for us. In the end, I learned a lesson to no longer plead incessantly with God when I am worried about things that haven't even happened yet. Instead, I try to pray prayers of faith, putting worries in God's hands, and letting him handle the outcome. You see, trust stops worry. Life is so much better that way, and I wonder if this simple truth is one key to experiencing God's provision.

Later, in the 1980s, Brenda and I moved north when I started school at North Central Bible College. There is more about how that unfolded in a later chapter. Once in Minneapolis, we would come under the teaching of Pastor Tom Elie at Praise Assembly. In that church Brenda and I felt unusually challenged to begin putting things into God's hands and letting go. The obvious benefit is that when you succeed in releasing a worry, you can step back and breathe easier. Even more importantly, the real bonus is that God now accepts responsibility for your problems, and it seems he has all kinds of amazing solutions at his disposal! Certainly, this was one time when he answered a prayer of fear indirectly with a simple lesson about faith, and his ability to provide.

Obey your parents

We rode that motorcycle 25,000 miles in about a year's time before it finally bit the dust. Along the way, the bike also yielded another experience that demonstrated God's intervention.

A coworker in my department was a Christian, and had become a good friend – and still is some forty years later. Darrell had purchased a motorcycle, but on an early outing lost control and slid into a curb. Since he was riding without a helmet, he was knocked out, and wound up in the emergency room. Afterward, his mother made him promise never to ride again.

However, during one summer when I lived near him I was giving him rides to work. One day, he got the urge to ride again, and his license was still valid. At his request, I allowed him to drive for the trip home. After a few miles, we came to a major intersection where highways 251 and 173 cross. As we entered the left turn lane I saw the longest and widest oil slick I have ever seen, before or since. Darrell was concentrating on making the light. However, I saw the oil and tried to warn him. But it was too late. As we entered the turn and braked, the wheels slid out from under us. Now this could have been very serious. But in this case, the oil allowed us to *slide* on the seats of our pants into the middle of the intersection, while the bike shot out ahead of us. We both got up unhurt and laughing.

The bike suffered a bent foot peg and damaged handle grip. Darrell's light colored corduroy jeans also were now black on the seat, but we were able to ride the bike the rest of the way to his mom's house. After that, to my knowledge, Darrell never rode again, but the bike still proved good for many more miles until finally the engine quit when one of the hotter plugs that I was running burned a hole in the cylinder, just as all the cycle experts had been warning me would happen!

If there is a lesson I learned from this it is that even when we do stupid things like letting someone else drive our vehicle, or in Darrell's case, ignoring his promise to his mother, God still loves us and is able to take care of us.

I have related this story because I believe that the hand of God was evident as it played out. That said, I don't really know why sometimes bad things happen in life, but I still have faith they are part of a plan that God has for each of us, and I believe someday we will understand the bigger picture when our time on earth is up. Both Jesus and Paul compared our temporary troubles to labor pains. Like labor pains, our troubles are small compared to the amazing potential outcomes such as the birth of a new child, or eternal life with Christ.

I brake for squirrels

I have always said that motorcycles are dangerous, and most bike owners I know have gone down on pavement or gravel at least once. This became the main reason Brenda and I sold our bike shortly before the birth of our first child. We wanted to be around to see our children grow up. We also knew that bikes really aren't ideal for family outings. Unfortunately, before that day came, I had to experience yet one more accident – an accident in which the hand of God was again evident.

The accident occurred after my first bike had died. My brother-in-law kindly offered to loan me a replacement. It was his mistake. I borrowed it to head north from Rockford on a hot day in the summer of 1980. The tar on Owen Center road was so hot that it was shiny. As I approached Highway 75 a squirrel ran out in front of me. I braked hard and immediately went down. My helmet hit the road and its foam left an impression on the left side of my face, not to mention a rather intense headache. After the fall, the bike wouldn't start, and I walked about two miles to a farmhouse to call for help.

By way of introduction, I have a long time friend who is also named Terry, thereby sharing my name. When he arrived with his bright yellow cargo van, we loaded the bike into it. Since the bike belonged to my brother-in-law, we dropped it off at his house, where my sister insisted I spend the night. She argued I might have a concussion and should be watched. So I stayed.

Unfortunately, that is not the end of the story. That evening, my sister was reading aloud a magazine article on the dangers of motorcycle riding. She read a statement that said that riders who owned bikes larger than 500 cc's for less then six months were those most likely to have an accident. She then said, "That sounds like Terry Light!" Terry had owned his Honda Goldwing for only a few months.

At almost that exact moment, the phone rang. My sister answered it, and I heard her say, "You are kidding, I know you, and you are kidding!" It was Terry on the other end of the line, but he wasn't kidding. He was telling her he had just been on his bike, and a car had changed lanes into him, forcing him off the road. After sliding along the curbing, he was now in the emergency room. The skin had been scraped off his forearm and leg. But Terry said that my accident had affected him, so this was the first time in a long time that he had worn a helmet. So on the same day, the two Terry's were in separate motorcycle accidents. The lesson for me was to not brake for squirrels, and to be cautious on hot tarry sections of roads. The lesson for Terry was to always wear a helmet.

But one has to ask, why did God even allow our

accidents in the first place? Why doesn't he simply protect us from harm? Those are tough questions, and I don't have a great answer, other than to say we won't always know the reasons things happen. I am always reminded of the verse that says, "All things work together for good for those who love God and are called according to His purpose." As often noted, God works in mysterious ways!

Vega Troubles

While we are on the subject of transportation, it would also be good to also talk about how God provided for Brenda and me around the time we were married. Besides a motorcycle, our other form of transportation was a less than ideal vehicle – a quirky green Chevy Vega. The gas gauge didn't work, which caused us to constantly monitor how many miles we had driven on each tank. Unfortunately, we often mis-calculated, but incredibly, this resulted in a series of little miracles. By our count the last five times in a row that the Vega ran out of gas we rolled right up to a gas pump before the car came to a stop!

Another story also involves the Vega. Sometimes God protects us even when we do stupid things. One of those stupid things I did involved this car. One day, the car didn't start because the fuel pump had stopped working. After carefully looking at a diagram of the car's layout in the owner's manual, I chiseled a hole about five inches in diameter through the middle of the trunk floor, thinking the pump would be right there as it was in the drawing. Instead, all I saw was another layer of sheet metal. At this point, I began chiseling another circle through that layer. I had gone four or five inches before I smelled gas, and realized I was chiseling into the gas tank! By God's grace, it did not spark an explosion, and I am still alive. Shaken, I found a mirror and used it to scope around where I had cut. The pump was actually off to one side, unlike the diagram! I then cut a hole in the correct place and replaced the pump. Finally, after epoxying the gas tank and patching the holes in the trunk with sheet metal, the car was like new – well, almost. It was a close call, and I thank God for letting me live another day.

* * *

*

CHAPTER 11

The Bus Flipped

When I first met Brenda, she was involved with a Campus Life group known as *Stateline Youth for Christ.* The group was led by Dick Myers at the time. Dick was an energetic individual with a talent for organizing creative events to bring high school kids together in Christian settings. Every year, Dick would organize a bus trip to Camp Forest Springs in Northern Wisconsin for several days of skiing, music, and special speakers.

On one such trip, Brenda and I were going as Campus Life staff. After packing our bus with sleeping bags and high school kids, we were ready to go. Dick led us in a prayer for safety and God's blessing. The bus then headed North. The trip was long, and we traveled almost the entire length of Wisconsin on the old Highway 51, passing through many small towns on snowy roads to reach the camp. But it was on the return trip that a little miracle became a memorable experience, and caused us to realize that God was with us.

After several days of skiing, singing, and listening to inspired speakers, we headed home. Gas stations were few, and eventually the bus driver slowed to turn in for gas. But what he thought was a right turn lane was actually just a ditch packed with snow that the plow blade had leveled. Suddenly, under the weight of the bus, the snow collapsed and the bus turned on its side.

Inside the bus, there was sudden panic. Kids screamed and fell over to our side, and Brenda and I became buried under other kids. When the panic subsided, we learned that the only injury was a girl's scraped thumb. Gradually, we made our way out the back emergency door. It was then that someone noted that unlike the trip north, we had not prayed for safety before the trip home! We reasoned that maybe God allowed this as a way of teaching us a small lesson.

But we were also about to see a little miracle. Here, in a remote section of highway in a forested area of northern Wisconsin, the bus flipped over directly in front of a semi-truck towing service! Within ninety minutes, a huge tow truck righted the bus and pulled it out of the ditch. Before we knew it, we were on our way home again, praising God for his provision!

Spiritual Warfare

A short time after Brenda and I were married, we allowed several individuals to share our home who needed a place to stay. One of those people was a single man struggling with alcohol and drug addiction. One day, Brenda and I returned from a shopping trip to find that he was in the attic of our two story home, working out with weights and listening to rock music on headphones. Brenda and I heard talking that sounded heated and emotional, and we listened in. As we did, we quickly realized that not all was well. We could only hear this young man's side of the conversation, but it sounded like he was was loudly arguing with demonic beings who were trying to kill him! He sounded quite distressed as he begged them to go away and leave him alone. Brenda and I immediately began to pray, and literally dropped to our knees asking God to intervene. We had only prayed a matter of seconds when suddenly, we heard him exclaim, "Thank you Jesus! Thank you Jesus!" Then, he came bounding down the attic stairs, ecstatic. When he saw us, he said, "You'll never guess what happened! I was working out, and demons started attacking me. But all of a sudden Jesus showed up in a long white robe and chased them all away!" So, while I have never been one to get worked up about the demonic realm, this experience convinced me it is real.

In the end, I believe that the Bible teaches that in Jesus there is deliverance available for any person trapped by demonic forces, and freedom comes through trusting in Jesus. I believe that when victory is finally realized, it generally comes through surrendering one's life to God's authority, and letting him deal with the powers of darkness.

* * *

*

CHAPTER 12

Life Lessons

Brenda and I did not grow in faith and maturity overnight, and we still have a ways to go. Some maturity may simply come with old age, but there have also been pastors and individuals who poured into our lives to build in us what God would want. I am going to mention some names in this chapter, because some of our friends reading this will share these memories, and can reminisce. I realize that others won't know them, but I don't apologize, because I believe that Pastoring is a challenging profession, and those who pour into the lives of others are deserving of more honor and recognition than I can give here.

In hindsight, I realize that God was only able to work in us through these individuals because we stayed closely connected to the body of Christ. For us, that connection primarily took place with churches, but also with our small Bible study group, a derivative of which still meets to this day.

At First Assembly, Pastor Moen brought in pastoral staff that became mentors who changed our lives and marriage for the better. You see, as a young Christian, I had some serious problems, and I think God had his hands full. Fortunately, we were going to the right church at the right time.

One of the things I struggled with was stubbornness. I was admittedly "stiff-necked." I knew this was the case, because God seemed to be repeatedly reminding me that this was true, and I came to know that the reason I was stiff-necked was because God was not able to lead me where he wanted due to my childhood dream of becoming a successful inventor. It was something he was going to have to work on during the next decades, and change did not come easily.

Another problem was that I feared the disapproval of others, and often couldn't say no to requests for my time or resources. Even yet another was that the words that came out of my mouth were often "worthless words," to quote Jeremiah 15:19. It seemed I would repeatedly stumble across that scripture in those days. I was also intensely introverted and prone to daily panic attacks in social situations, which reminds me that the other verse I seemed to stumble upon on almost a daily basis was, "Do not fear, for I am with you." Isaiah 41:10 is the reference, and it was apparently something I needed to hear. Doubt was also an issue I wrestled with from time to time in those days, as I drifted between skepticism and faith. It probably didn't help that I had read books written by skeptics who wrote about topics I was interested in, such as world hunger, politics, and science, and had subscribed to a rather liberal Christian magazine for several years. On a lighter note, I won't talk about the lessons Brenda had to learn. If she wants to express that, she will have to write her own book. :)

During this time in my life, I needed to find healing in these areas, and there were pastors at First Assembly who made a difference. When Brenda and I were dating, we were attending the College and Career class on Sunday mornings. Pastor Dale Crall was only three years older than myself, and led the class. He had a special calling from God to minister to young people, and he dealt with my skeptical nature quite effectively, helping my faith to grow.

We absolutely loved the testimonies he told of how God had worked, and was continuing to work in his life. In fact, one of my main motivations for writing this book has been memories of the effect Dale's testimonies had on my own faith. Recently, I learned that Dale is still active today at Southern Illinois University, and he is still ministering to college age students.

It is not only testimonies that God can use to change lives. There were also others at First Assembly who also influenced me as a young Christian. Pastor David Ytterock was my teacher for a Public Speaking class at the Bible school. When I gave a speech on the vastness of the universe, he challenged me that the speech lacked meaningful purpose. I saw he was right, and his comment painfully confirmed what I had been hearing from God, that I had a problem with not speaking noble words that made a difference. It is a lesson I have not forgotten, especially as I attempt to minister to others by writing books.

Around this time Brenda and I had been dating for about two years, and we set a date to be married. As part of standard protocol at First Assembly, we went through marriage counseling. Another pastor on staff, Pastor Dan Wilderman, counseled us and ultimately married us. I still remember much of his advice, and it apparently worked. As I write this, Brenda and I have now been married 37 years.

In the months after we were married Brenda and I let a few individuals move into our house. One young woman had a problem with creating elaborate lies, and I was gullible enough to believe her some of the time. In fact, I could easily devote an entire chapter to the drama surrounding this girl. But suffice it to say that shortly after she moved in, Dale Crall pulled me aside and told me that if I valued my reputation, I should distance myself from her. To this day I am not sure what she told him concerning me, but I was naive and resisted his advice. And she wasn't the only problem person in our home.

A couple of the guys also had problems with alcohol, drugs, and honesty. And most were not employed. Yet somehow, I thought that if we extended trust to these individuals they would change.

One memorable message became a turning point for me while we were attending the Young Married classes led by Pastor John Davis. Pastor John began a message by asking, "How many think that it is okay for Christians to be gullible?" Of course, I assumed it was a trick question. Obviously the Christian thing to do was to trust people, so I raised my hand along with others. But we were quickly shown the error of our thinking according to scripture. Jesus told his followers to be as wise as serpents, but harmless as doves. Paul told us not to be unequally yoked with unbelievers, and to separate ourselves from those who claim to follow Christ, but do not.

This was a message I had heard before, but this time it really connected. It became a turning point which soon led to a confrontation with this girl about her lies, and ultimately led to us kicking her out of our home. It was a tough time, but good came from it in the end, and now I try to be a little more discerning. Others continued to live in our home, but things would change radically soon, for a clean break with Rockford was in the works. God was getting ready to move us to Minnesota.

Alive

The seed for the move to Minneapolis was actually planted months ahead of time. On a Saturday night I was driving past Sinnissippi Park in Rockford. As I drove I was praying, asking God to help me find something worthwhile to become involved in. Although I was attending Bible School, something still seemed to be missing. About this time, I noticed a broken piece of sign lying on the road ahead. As I passed over it I saw it had the lone word "Alive" painted on it. And then, at that exact moment the DJ on the radio said "alive." This grabbed my attention, and as I listened I realized the voice on the radio was promoting "Youth Alive," a ministry starting up at our church. I thought it strange, and I wondered if that meant God might be asking me to become involved with Youth Alive, but I recall thinking I would never volunteer.

But God had other plans. The next morning at church, Brenda and I attended Pastor John's class. Afterwards, we were approached in the hall and asked if we would be willing to help out in the Youth Alive program! To Brenda's surprise, I said "Yes" without hesitation, because God had literally given me a sign :). Of course, I hadn't mentioned the sign to Brenda, and didn't consult with her before answering the question, so at first she protested. But I explained, and she got on board, and we began to help out with youth meetings.

Minneapolis Bound

In the Youth Alive program we were helping Pastor Jerry Greene, who was the youth pastor. Our involvement then led to even more evidence of God's plan for us. This sense that working with high school kids wasn't my strong suit just intensified the feeling for me that we needed to find where we really fit in. I also was working fifty hour weeks, which, coupled with my inability to get a restful night's sleep, left me feeling like I needed a change.

So one Wednesday afternoon I was at work making springs when I began to ponder the option of moving to another city to attend one of the Bible colleges associated with our denomination. North Central Bible College in Minneapolis came to mind, but I was also aware of other options such as Central Bible College that were farther away. It wasn't the first time I had considered this idea, but on this day it came to a head.

Now I insert here that I don't necessarily think college is for everyone. Nor can I say that it is for no one. It is something that must be prayed about, and a person needs to go where God leads, because God's plan is different for every person. And that is precisely what I attempted to do. Before leaving work that day, I asked God if he would give me a sign that very same day – before bedtime – one way or the other.

And God answered in what seemed to be an incredible way. At the Wednesday night Youth Alive meeting, Pastor Jerry Greene asked us if Brenda and I would be available to chaperone a bus filled with youth on a trip to visit North Central Bible College! Immediately I knew this was the sign I had asked for, and of course said "Yes," once again without consulting Brenda, and once again having to explain after the fact that I had asked God for a sign earlier that day.

During our visit to North Central, Brenda and I sat next to a couple, Bob and Faye, who were already students there. Through their encouragement, Brenda's fears were allayed, and I became more certain of what I already thought I knew – that God was calling us there. When I returned to work I gave my employer six months notice. As it turned out, I ended up working for Woodward Governor exactly ten years and two weeks.

That summer, Brenda and I put our house on the market. It would be months before it sold, which seemed distressing at the time. Then we donated most of our things, and packed the remaining ones rather tightly into a VW bus. Finally, in early September of 1983 we moved to Minneapolis, feeling a little sad to leave family and friends behind, but also excited about the future.

Miracle Blanket

Minneapolis was an unfamiliar city, and we felt both fear and awe when we arrived. After nearly a week-long search, we found one of the few apartments that would allow a dog, but we had to lower our standards. It did not have a working elevator, and it took three days to haul the contents of our van up to the third floor apartment. Yet God seemed to be in it, for the rent was low and it was only a five minute walk to school, allowing Brenda to use the car to find employment. Meanwhile, I focused on getting good grades, and we lived off my former job's retirement fund payout. And then we experienced a small miracle.

We had arrived just in time for a Minnesota cold snap, and it quickly became apparent that the apartment's heat wasn't working. The building manager said the boiler needed repair, and it would be a couple days before it was fixed. That night we were so cold it seemed like pure torture.

The next day, we decided to purchase an electric blanket. Normally that would not have been a problem. After classes, we headed to K-mart, but the cheapest electric blanket cost a few dollars more than the cash in our pockets. To make matters worse, our bank had already closed, and in this age before debit cards, K-mart's service desk wouldn't approve our bank's starter checks. Feeling desperate, Brenda and I wandered back to the blanket aisle. With nowhere else to turn, we decided to pray. We held hands and I whispered a prayer asking God to keep us warm.

Then we headed for the car. As we neared the main entrance we crossed paths with a man I recognized from five years earlier and 300 miles south. It was someone we had met when street witnessing in Illinois, and who had then attended Galilee House Coffeehouse.

On this day he had obviously been drinking. I said, "Hi Don," and got his attention. As soon as he recognized me, he pulled a ten dollar bill from his pocket and tried to thrust it into my hand, all the while saying loudly and repeatedly, "Take this, I owe you!" We refused the money at first, but he was persistent, and we finally accepted it. We thanked him profusely, and told him it was a huge answer to prayer, which was a truth I doubt he could fully appreciate. We then returned to the back of the store and picked up a twin-size electric blanket, which was enough to keep us warm for a couple nights until the building's heat came on.

As I remember this, it amazes me. Who would ever think that such an instant answer to prayer was even possible? Somehow, God must have planned ahead of time to put a man in our path we already knew in a strange city, and then motivate him to meet a need he didn't even know existed. It is no wonder that people in the Bible concluded that God was all-powerful. So in spite of our doubts, lack of understanding, and lack of faith, which Christians everywhere have to wrestle with from time to time, God is still able to act in amazing ways in response to prayer.

* * *

*

CHAPTER 13

Three Fires

One night around midnight, as we slept in our third floor apartment, we were awakened by sirens, spotlights, and a loud-speaker telling us to remain in the building. The street below was lined with fire trucks. Everything worked out okay, and we later learned that a cooking fire on the floor below ours had prompted the alarm. But that was just the first of three fires.

When I arrived at school, I learned that at about the same time as our fire, a fire had also occurred in the school's dormitory because a student left a hair dryer running. That fire also did not cause a lot of damage. And then, in the student assembly that day we learned that also during that same night there was yet another fire, and it was a big one. It caused the First Assembly of God church in Detroit to burn to the ground.

There were three fires in one night. What significance do I give this you might ask? On the surface it seems to be a strange coincidence, and I have trouble finding any deep meaning in it. I certainly don't believe God is in the business of starting fires just to create coincidences. But I do believe that God allows things to happen, and changes the timing of things for reasons only he knows. I believe that coincidences can let Christians know that God loves is, is here with us, and wants to point us to where he is leading. They have done all of that for me in the past. So if I may speculate, possibly the only reason for such a coincidence was to increase the faith of the students at North Central Bible College, and the only reason for allowing the fire in my building might have been simply because he knew this story would someday wind up in a book!

By the end of that first year of college, our cash had dwindled. Brenda was working at McDonalds, and I began looking for a job to get us through the summer. Answering ads and knocking on doors seemed to take forever. It eventually resulted in a job at a local machine shop. By summer's end they offered me the position of Production Engineer, and asked me to consider not going back to school. With funds tight, it seemed the only real option. So I continued to work in this company for the next four years.

It was a high stress job that demanded long hours but provided good income. We bought a house a block away, and Brenda switched to Taco Bell where she was promoted to Assistant Manager. And this was before kids. My sister called us a DINK couple – Double Income No Kids! So obviously these were years of plenty. Yet all the while, I realized that I was tired and stressed, and never felt rested in the mornings. Usually, when I woke up, I would experience a sense of dread, until I consumed caffeine. Then, I would gradually feel better as the day wore on. I also would experience nervousness, frequent panic attacks, and an overall sense of tiredness. Then, by evening I would be wide awake, and ready to stay up all night. I was convinced I needed a miracle, and continued to pray for healing. But it would still be another decade before healing would come.

Lessons on I90

While we lived in Minneapolis, we would make trips on almost all holidays to the Illinois-Wisconsin state line to visit family and friends. Of course, these trips were often in winter. On one snowy return trip we were in heavy traffic when we passed a stalled car with an elderly couple inside. A white handkerchief had been tied to the antenna. We concluded that they most likely had run out of gas, but in seconds we were already too far past to pull over. We talked about circling back, but it seemed the extra interstate miles would be difficult. So we continued on and prayed that someone else would help. I assumed that this was the end of that, but God had something else in mind.

About two hundred miles later as darkness fell, we also ran out of gas. After digging a gas can out of the trunk I stood beside the road and put out a thumb, hoping for a lift. But no one stopped. I finally got back in the car to stay warm, but even in the car it was cold.

Of course, it was difficult not to connect our own misfortune with the earlier decision not to return to help the elderly couple. As we sat there, I wondered aloud if we would spend the same amount of time in the cold waiting for help as they had! In all, it was about ninety minutes that we sat waiting, all the while staring at a road sign in front of the car. Printed on the sign were the words, "Black River Falls, 1/4 mile."

The words became burned into our brains. We couldn't realize at the time how meaningful that sign would become. Eventually a state trooper stopped and called for roadside assistance. Soon, we were back on the road, but that is not the end of the story.

On the same return leg of our next trip we came upon a car with a flat tire. Remembering our previous experience, I pulled in behind them to offer help. It was a family in an older model car, and they were genuinely stranded for lack of a spare tire. Fortunately, I had a can of tire sealant which inflated their tire enough to drive on. And then we prepared to follow them to a gas station.

But as we got back into our car an amazing thing happened. It was then that Brenda and I noticed in amazement the sight before us. We could hardly believe that we hadn't seen it right away, but this family had been staring at the same Black River Falls road sign in front of them that had been in front of us when *we* were stranded. It was almost as if God was saying, "Yes, I gave you a second chance, and because of your obedience I am blessing you by letting you see my hand in this situation."

Still, I would not want to limit the scope of this miracle to the little world that Brenda and I share. Surely, this was also a miracle for the stranded family. At a moment of extreme stress, Brenda and I showed up to lend a helping hand, which was also likely an answer to a prayer that they prayed, and a lesson on God's faithfulness for them. I like to believe that God had purposes for all of us that were fulfilled by this simple act of obedience.

This Dream is Prophetic

In the summer of 1988, a planned vacation had us meeting friends from Illinois for a week of camping at Wisconsin Dells. Before the trip, I built a pontoon boat out of plastic barrels and treated wood, and modified a utility trailer to haul it. When we arrived at the Dells, it was unfinished and took half of our vacation just to get it into the water. I am sure the other campers appreciated the sound of power tools! The hard work ultimately paid off with a few boat trips. On the first trip there were twelve of us on board – kids included – when waves from a passing tour boat swamped our deck. I prayed hard that the boats construction would hold, and thankfully it did.

Brenda driving the pontoon boat – eyes closed, and no hands!

The boat's big problem was that it had a used motor. After a few trips, the motor quit, stranding us a long ways from home at midnight in a dense fog with one passenger experiencing flue symptoms. We ended up paddling all the way back to camp, and felt fortunate just to find our dock in the fog. So a vacation that was supposed to be fun and relaxing ended up filled with hard work and danger.

Yet, in spite of the difficulties, I felt tremendous relief to be away from the stress of work. Brenda also felt relief, and longed to move closer to family and friends. So it was on this vacation that we made the decision we would quit our jobs in one year and move back to Illinois.

When vacation was over, we gave notice to our employers. I was glad to tell mine well in advance because I was involved in a costly design project, and wanted a smooth transition. And then about two weeks before my quit date, I had a vivid dream.

In the dream, Brenda and I were driving in our car with some friends past a row of houses. Out of a chimney of a two-story brick house came a snake made of smoke, which found its way through the back window of the car and then bit me in the back of my neck. We then drove to the corner and turned right. I was afraid that snakes might come out of other chimneys also, but somehow I knew that turning the corner meant that this would never happen again. At that point, I awoke in pitch darkness in the middle of the night and found myself saying with authority, "This dream is prophetic, and it will come to pass." I thought, "Wow – that's amazing. I've never had a dream like that. I'll have to remember it." But I promptly fell back to sleep.

But then, as morning approached, I had the same exact dream all over again, with all the same details. And again, I awoke saying, "This dream is prophetic, and it will come to pass." But this time, instead of darkness, I awoke in bright daylight and immediately realized I had had two identical dreams! The dreams made quite an impression and I decided to spend a little time praying and reading my Bible before getting ready for work. As I opened my ASV study Bible, the first verse I saw was this one in Proverbs:

> "The north wind brings forth rain: so does a backbiting tongue an angry countenance." (Proverbs 25:23)

The verse was talking about gossip. It was easy to see see that the backbiting snake made out of smoke might be a picture of gossip. Like smoke, gossip is not a physical threat. With that, I could do little more than wonder if it might be fulfilled anytime soon, so I got ready for work.

I didn't have to wait long. When I got to work, I was told that I had been fired. The timing was about two weeks before the quit date I had given. At home, we immediately rented a U-Haul and began packing.

A day or so later I stopped by the shop and learned my former employer had been told that we would move to Illinois on the quit date we had told him, even if the project I was working on was not at a transition point. I told him that this was not true. I intended all along to stay as long as it took to finish that portion of the project I was working on, even though I knew this might mean staying more weeks or months before we could move. He then offered my job back.

But we were already half-packed, so I declined. In fact, getting fired was actually a blessing, for it allowed us to make the move without the entanglement of waiting for a break in my work. So even though I felt emotional shock, the dream said to me that God cared about us and was directing our steps.

The move took two trips, and resulted in our being stranded in Wisconsin for three nightmarishly long days when the pontoon boat's trailer broke. The events might have seemed hilarious if they weren't so tragic. A flat tire resulted in a cracked rim which turned out to be obsolete. This meant the entire axle had to be replaced. Yet no axles of the correct length could be found that would fit between the boat's pontoons. So in the end it took three days to modify a new axle and install it while we remained stranded beside the interstate. I recall it was really hard at the time to see God's hand in this, and at least one time as we worked late into the night, we were practically in tears. But we eventually made it to Illinois, where we were welcomed into a community living situation with the two couples we had vacationed with.

* * *

CHAPTER 14

Divine Appointment in Canada

When we first arrived in Rockford, I began looking for work, and eventually accepted a job at a large company. But, when the economy declined and a layoff brought that to an end a year later, I became serious about starting my own business. A friend put me in touch with someone who needed help building automated machines. He and I informally became business partners, although we never shared the same perspective regarding faith in God. I was clearly unequally yoked in this situation. But still, the job provided a rather erratic source of income and some valuable job experience.

One order we received was for creating a press attachment for the company in Ottawa that prints Canada's currency. We proceeded to design and build the machine, and loaded it into Dave's pickup truck for the trip north. Upon arrival, it took more than a week to complete the installation. During that time, I became casually acquainted with a woman who ran the press next to the one we were working on. Her name was Barb, and she was about twenty years my senior.

That Sunday, I picked a church out of the motel phone book and attended their service. When I arrived, it had a large auditorium that probably seated well over a thousand people. At first it looked completely packed, but then I spotted two empty chairs toward the front. One had a Bible on it, so I asked about it. Someone said they thought the other chair was vacant, so I sat down. A few minutes later the Bible's owner returned, and I was surprised to see that it was Barb. Here in a large church in the middle of a big city was a familiar face. It seems God had arranged for me to sit with one of the few people I had met in Canada.

After the service, Barb shared with me the difficulties she faced living with a husband who wouldn't attend church, and I shared the difficulties I faced working with a partner who openly rejected God. Then we prayed together. I genuinely believe that it was a God-orchestrated meeting.

Stranded in the Cold

Once the installation of the machine was complete, Dave and I began the return trip home. We planned on driving non-stop through the night, but the road between Ottawa and Toronto was long, lined with snow, and desolate. To make matters worse, gas stations were few and far between. When the gauge reached a quarter tank we began looking for gas. With still no station in sight, the needle touched "Empty," and we began imagining the worst. It was then we saw a sign for a town two miles off the highway. Exiting we found that the town was no more than a couple houses at an intersection. We turned right rather than head back, thinking we would be better off if we ran out of gas near a farmhouse than on the interstate.

Soon afterward, we did indeed run out of gas. It could have been tragic, except for a tiny miracle. As we rolled to a stop, we found that we were right in front of a small building with a sign declaring it was a Royal Canadian Mounted Police station. The building was dark, but we pounded on the glass door, and an officer in his pajamas showed up. He made us wait outside in the cold while he put on a uniform, after which he took us to a truck stop so we could make arrangements to get back on the road. At the Truck stop, we filled a gas can and tried to hitch-hike back to Dave's truck, but without luck.

It was then that I noticed a problem. The cold had dropped my core body temperature to the point that I began having great difficulty walking and talking. Dave agreed that

I could go inside to warm up, and he would continue to look for a ride. Once inside, I sat down at a counter and tried to order a hot cup of coffee, but the waitress thought I was drunk. I told her I was just cold, but she refused to have anything to do with me. Fortunately, after a while Dave came back. He had found a willing trucker, and before long we were back on the road. In spite of our mistakes God protected us, and I became wiser about filling gas tanks more frequently when driving in desolate regions.

I also gained a new appreciation for how easy it is to misjudge others. I had just experienced what it feels like to be ostracized based on appearances, and it is a lesson I try not to forget when meeting those the world has judged to fall short of their standards.

* * *

*

CHAPTER 15

Sunday School Decision

The panic attacks I would often experience on a daily basis were fairly severe. They most often occurred in social situations, though sometimes even when I was alone. My face would turn red, eyes would water, and I would feel like I was choking. It was often quite embarrassing. I had found various ways of countering the effect by clenching my toes or pinching my leg, but it still caused me to avoid most social interaction. The healing would finally come indirectly over a period of time in the form of wisdom, and as a direct answer to a rather unusual prayer.

Our pastor, James Moore of Riverside Assembly, had told his own testimony how God had stretched him and led him until finally he became a pastor. It all began, however, when he volunteered to teach Sunday School. I thought that I too would like to teach Sunday School, but I was sure it could never happen, due to the panic attacks. So I made a deal with God. I told him that if he would take the panic attacks away from me, I would volunteer to teach.

The answer seemed to come almost immediately. I went until the next Sunday without a panic attack, so I volunteered. However, the success seemed short lived, because soon after, the attacks came back. Yet it seemed that God had given me a sign, so I stuck to my commitment. But now, as I was thrust weekly in front of a class of first and second graders, I began to even more seriously pray for answers. As a result, I began to experiment with various natural supplements. It wasn't long before I found my sleep and energy levels improved to the point that the panic attacks were finally gone for good. Since then, as God has stretched me with additional teaching opportunities. In general, being stretched in this way has helped my nerves improve when standing in front of an audience. Looking back, I consider this simple decision to volunteer to teach to be a major turning point in my life.

A Call to Write

When I was young, I never dreamed of being a writer, and equated writing with homework, which I despised. It seemed tedious, even though I seemed to do well on the rare occasions when I actually turned writing assignments in. But my passion was to be an engineer.

As I grew older, I began to sense a desire to influence others. In the 1970s, I even submitted a Christian article to the Overflowing Cup Coffeehouse in Beloit, which they published in their monthly newsletter. Still, writing it seemed tedious. So when they asked me for more articles, I am a little ashamed to say that I turned down the invitation. But God had other plans. After moving back to Illinois we began attending Riverside Assembly, a church on the northwest edge of Rockford, where James Moore was pastor.

One service in particular was especially meaningful. A visiting evangelist was speaking to a full house about the importance of every Christian finding a ministry that God was calling them to. He stressed that most Christians were not called to preach, but that God has a plan for each and every one of us. As he spoke, I asked God, "What ministry do you have for me – do you want me to write?" At that instant, the evangelist looked directly at me, and he said, "God is calling some of you to be writers!" He then looked around the room and named other professions such as doctors and lawyers in similar fashion. But now God had my attention. I was as startled as if God himself had just told me, "I want you to write!"

So this began a process in which I began to wrestle

with all of my excuses for not writing, which primarily centered around my dream of being an engineer. Yet writing did seem to be in sync with what I had been hearing from God through the years. I had always sensed a desire to do something meaningful with my faith related to ministry, but now it seemed God had finally clarified my calling, and the focus was writing.

Miracle Job Search

But before I could pour myself into writing, I still needed to earn a living. Brenda and I also needed to experience other aspects of God's plan for us. So writing had to wait. For three years I was self-employed designing automated machines. For our family these were times of feast and famine. Large checks were usually followed by long periods without pay, and the more routine computer services I was providing weren't bringing in enough to pay bills during lean times.

In hindsight, I was not in the center of God's will when I ignored the obvious need to get a job as I pursued the dream of self-employment, if I had it to do over again common sense would suggest I develop my dream on the side. Eventually, Brenda and I agreed it was time to get a real job, so I launched a job search.

Random?

One day, in order to obtain a list of prospective employers, I went to the library and looked up businesses in the local Chamber of Commerce directory. There were literally hundreds to choose from, most of which had nothing to do with my experience. After writing down the addresses of a few large manufacturers that seemed like real possibilities, I decided to give God a chance by picking two more companies completely at random. I was pleasantly surprised that they were both machine shops, and I was even more surprised that one of them already knew me, because I and my partner had done some work for them in the past. In fact, they had also made some parts for me. More specifically, the two companies were United Tool, and Blackhawk Machine. It was Blackhawk that already knew me.

I didn't have much faith in random picks, so at first I applied at all the bigger companies I had chosen using my own wisdom. But none of them even offered me an interview, let alone a job. Finally, I had only the two random picks left, and both of them gave me interviews! And then, a second little miracle – Blackhawk offered me a job! Since then, I have told this story a number of times to Sunday school classes as a testimony of God's guidance and provision. What seemed random at the time was apparently not random from God's perspective. But that is not the end of the story.

When this book was almost complete the story developed another little miracle twist. Remember United, the first random pick that interviewed me 25 years earlier without hiring me? A father and son team who work for United started their own company on the side a few years ago and called it Seraph Industries. They used United's facilities to begin making pellet stoves, and then they expanded to building bigger machines that make the pellets. Very recently, Seraph bought Blackhawk because Blackhawk had been making many of their parts. So while I still work for Blackhawk in the same building, I now report to people who still work for United, but under the name Seraph – a name which was not in existence when I applied at United. In other words, in a way, I now work for both random picks as part of God's plan for my life! It seems that sometimes God has amazing ways of letting us know that he is the master planner, and that he is even in control of the tiny details!

Roof on the Front Lawn

After finding the job at Blackhawk, Brenda and I bought a house from my father where I had lived from fifth grade until after I found a job. It was a very windy Saturday, and my dad was visiting. We were standing in the family room, talking about home remodeling. My dad knew that we were living paycheck to paycheck, but he said, "You know, one of these days you are going to have to replace this leaky roof." I agreed with him, but even before the words left my mouth a loud roar interrupted our conversation. Behind where I was standing, the stovepipe shot up through the ceiling, leaving a gaping hole with blue sky above it. We ran outside, and could see that the pipe and roofing were gone, but we could not see where they landed. Walking around the house, we found the roofing material and stovepipe laying on the front lawn. It was a real mess.

In the end, insurance bought a professionally installed new roof for the back two-thirds. I still wound up shingling the front one-third myself, but friends from church came out, and together we completed it on a Saturday morning. My dad is in his 90s, and he still remembers this story fondly. That roof worked great for the next twenty years, and then was destroyed in another amazing twist when trees fell on it. But more about that later.

Nostradamus a Christian?

Through these years, I did not forget that God had called me to write. But in order to write one must choose a topic. The early years of my writing were quite exploratory, and I began to dabble in different topics. All along I felt inexperienced and out of my league. But to gain practice, I became more intentional about keeping a journal. It is something I had already been doing for decades, but now I became more consistent.

About this time, I developed an interest in Nostradamus, the French astrologist, so I began to write what I thought was a Christian perspective of the writings of Nostradamus. Gradually, I had accumulated enough material to put into book form.

Now I can just hear some of you mumbling, so let me assure you that I am not particularly proud of this excursion into the occult. However, I rationalized that because Nostradamus claimed allegiance to Christ I could do this with a clear conscience. I actually think that God was letting me try out my new directive in a sandbox where I was free to make mistakes, before kicking me out into the real world.

After three years of hard work on a book about Nostradamus, I carefully printed the best chapters which I then submitted to seven publishing houses. Gradually, one by one, I received rejections. After six rejections, only one response had not yet been received.

It was only then, on a Saturday morning, that I thought I heard clearly from God that I was not supposed to publish the book. Over and over again, during the next few hours it seemed that everywhere I looked God was telling me not to publish the book. Even people on TV seemed to be saying "Don't publish that book!"

Finally, feeling somewhat defeated, I approached Brenda and told her the news. Her response was, "How on earth can you think of giving up on this when you have invested so much time and effort?" But I was so confident that it was God who was speaking to me that I made a deal with her. I said that if she could pick a random verse out of any Bible in the house that had nothing to do with the evils of astrology, I would go ahead and publish the book. She seemed to think such a deal was good, since there are only a couple verses in the Bible that even deal with astrology. So she quickly grabbed a Bible and opened it. Then, putting her finger down she began to read aloud. After about two words Brenda looked up in disbelief and said simply, "You're not supposed to publish the book."

A few minutes later I went out to the mailbox. In it was a letter from the seventh publisher, saying that they would like to publish the book if I was up to putting in some hard work. It was with some sadness that I responded saying I no longer wanted to publish it. Since then, I have not stopped writing, but have gone on to self-publish several other books on topics which are far less controversial from a Christian perspective, of which this is the fourth.

With the Nostradamus book, God allowed me to learn important lessons as I created and submitted a manuscript. And then, in the final moments he pulled the plug. In the middle of great disappointment, we were in awe of his split-second timing.

* * *

*

CHAPTER 16

Godslist

Around the year 1998, Brenda's aunt gave us a car, and we decided we needed to sell our other car, which was an older Plymouth Horizon. At church one Sunday morning, we asked our adult class to pray that God would help us sell the car, and we told them we would list it in the paper. But God had different plans.

When we pulled into our driveway after church, our friends prayers had already put things in motion. To our amazement there was a Hispanic family of five standing in the front yard. After introductions, the father asked us if we had a car for sale. I answered in the affirmative, and asked them how they knew. They said they noticed that the car in the driveway did not have license plates. They somehow concluded that this meant it was for sale!

I quickly pointed out that the one in the driveway was not the one for sale. Instead, it was the one we were driving. Soon we had negotiated a price and completed the transaction. The next Sunday, I had a great testimony to share with our Sunday morning class. I have only rarely been more amazed at how quickly God can answer a prayer!

Balloon Coincidence

Hot air balloons are a rare sight in our city. But on one warm summer day when our kids were young, the wind died and a hot air balloon became stalled over our neighbors' house. After much time passed, it finally landed in our neighbor's driveway. I snapped a picture as our sons stood watching, and showed the picture to our Sunday school class.

Our sons watch a balloonist after he landed by our lawn.

Eventually, a crowd gathered and watched as the balloon was loaded into a truck. Soon, however, not to be outdone, a couple in our Sunday school class also had a balloon encounter when one landed in their backyard. It's as if God has a sense of humor. Even though it seemed hard to find any deeper meaning, the landings seemed funny, and it did result in a great Sunday morning discussion on the subject of coincidences!

Ketchup Coincidence

Culture has always been a lofty goal for me, as evidenced by a love for blue jeans and avoidance of fine restaurants. But still, even I find this next story a bit embarrassing. One day, after a stop at McDonalds I went to Menards to pick up a few things. On the way to the car, I noticed a large vertical slop of ketchup on my cream colored polo shirt, a mess that had certainly been glaringly obvious to the checkout clerk and others. The only fix was a trip home, and a change of shirts.

I wish I could say that that was the end of the story. The next morning, our local Christian radio station asked people to call in with their favorite pet peeves. A woman called in to say her pet peeve was when a "decent looking guy wears a nice polo shirt with ketchup down the front." Of course I was sure she was talking about me, and I was embarrassed! The blow was softened slightly by the words "decent looking," but as my wife and others seem too quick to point out, she did not say "great looking!" Wouldn't it be a funny coincidence if the person who called the radio station that day would someday read this?

A Child Near Death

One Sunday morning in our church service, Brenda and I learned that the daughter of a couple in our class was in a life or death struggle. Callie, their little girl, had been diagnosed with pneumonia, and was listed in serious condition. We prayed for her, and trusted God to heal her, but on Wednesday night at the mid-week prayer service we were told she was in critical condition and might not last the night. So those of us in the Wednesday evening service gathered around the front and knelt at the altar to pray.

I felt devastated by the possibility that this little girl might die, so the next day I determined to fast until such a time as I heard that Callie was okay. On my lunch break, I didn't eat, but used the time to pray and read my Bible. By the end of the lunch break I felt I had a confirmation that Callie would be okay, and I returned to work encouraged. At this time I admit I broke my fast with junk food from the snack box, which was not very satisfying. When I arrived home, I was delighted to learn that suddenly on Wednesday evening, Callie had surprised everyone by taking a turn for the better. By the next morning she was so healthy it was as though she had never been sick. So the timing suggested that our prayer service was indeed effective, and my additional fasting and prayer may have been unnecessary. I have often recalled this answer to prayer when I pray for people who are sick, or when I begin to feel like things are hopeless.

As I mentioned before, James recognized the dynamic that prayer has when followers of Christ pray for each other. He instructs us to "confess your sins to each other and pray for each other so that you may be healed. The prayer of a righteous person is powerful and effective." (James 5:16, NIV). Jesus also alluded to the amazing power of prayer when believers gather together. He said, "Again, truly I tell you that if two of you on earth agree about anything they ask for, it will be done for them by my Father in heaven." (Matthew 18:19, NIV). This is certainly the dynamic that seems to have been in operation the day God healed Callie.

* * *

CHAPTER 17

Kids in Danger

One afternoon on a weekend, I was taking a nap when I suddenly woke up alarmed, convinced that our three sons, aged 6 to 10, were in serious danger. I raced to the front room and looked out the window, only to see our sons on the front stoop talking with a neighbor kid. Nothing seemed out of the ordinary, so I opened the door a crack and listened. An older teenager from down the street had their undivided attention, and was telling them that the gay lifestyle was wonderful and fulfilling. Immediately, I opened the door wide and told the boy with strong words to leave and not come back. I strongly believe that God intervened in this situation because of our prayers for the safety of our kids, and in doing so protected them from a situation where sexual abuse would have been likely.

A Supernatural Connection

Mike was a fellow employee who often vocalized his belief in the non-existence of God. One day after work, we entered into a discussion in the parking lot. During the course of the conversation Mike stated, "In my entire life I have never experienced a single event that I would consider supernatural, or even mysterious." I said, "Well I'm going to pray that you do." And so I did. The next day, Mike was giving me a hand at the parts washer, when suddenly I felt a sensation of panic, as though I was drowning. I gasped, and when Mike asked what was wrong, I told him what I had felt. I noted the time and said, "I have never felt such a feeling before. I'm going to ask around and see if anyone I know had something happen to them at 9:50 am."

That evening when I arrived home, I asked Brenda,

"Did anything unusual happen today?" She replied, "No, not really." So I asked more questions, "How about something scary?" Then she said, "As a matter of fact, I went to a tanning place and the door on the tanning bed jammed and I wasn't able to get out. I kind of panicked, but then when I pushed really hard it opened, and everything was okay." So I asked, "About what time would you say that was?" I avoided leading her in any way. She said, "Well, I left the one place about 9:30 and got to the tanning place about 9:45." So I asked, "*Exactly* what time then do you think the door jammed?" She was rather puzzled why I would even care, but then she said, "I would guess it was about five minutes after I got there, or about ten minutes to ten."

The next day, I relayed to Mike our conversation, but I could see he didn't believe a word of it, apparently thinking I must have fabricated the entire story for his benefit, so I let it drop. However, about a year or so later, another experience also involved Mike.

Coincidence Marathon

It began on a Sunday morning when in the course of teaching a class I commented that coincidences often are signs from God that let us know he is with us and loves us. I also mentioned in the same class that Brenda and I had been using firewood to cut our heating costs, and mentioned that we needed firewood, if anyone happened to know of any. Someone in the class must have prayed for us, because that afternoon, when we arrived home from church, there was a trailer loaded with firewood parked in our driveway. Ben, a landscaper who did not attend out church had cut down a tree for a customer and thought he might be able to dispose of the wood by giving it to us.

Later that day and during the next there were several more "coincidences." They were less significant than the firewood, but still I was recording each in my journal. The sudden cluster seemed quite unusual. I continued to note coincidences over the next several days. By Thursday, I had documented fourteen "coincidences," so I decided to share my list with my skeptic friend Mike. Just as I finished reading the list, Gina came out from the office. In the noisy machine shop she was completely unaware of our conversation, but said excitedly, "Guess what happened yesterday? We had a bill where we owed a large amount of money, and I had no idea how we were going to pay it. So, I prayed about it. Then yesterday, when I went out to the mailbox, there was an unexpected check for exactly that amount of money. It was a miracle!"

Mike emphatically commented, "It wasn't a miracle!" So I chipped in, "Look, here I am, sharing a list of fourteen coincidences, when Gina stops by and shares an amazing "coincidence" of her own. That in itself is another amazing coincidence. These aren't just coincidences, but God wants to tell you that he is real." To this Mike replied, "The reality is that both of you are living in some sort of other reality – a Terry reality." And then he walked away, and that was the end of that, except that I then told Gina what we had just been talking about before she came out. I still have that journal with all the coincidences, and whenever I stumble across it, it is a most refreshing read for it reminds me that not only is God with us, but he loves us and wants to reveal himself to us.

I often think about events like these when I run into people who are rejecting God. To me such happenings are evidence that God is calling people everywhere to himself, and offering them a gift of faith if they can only find the spiritual strength to break free from the chains of skepticism and accept it.

* * *

*

CHAPTER 18

Three Cardinal Signs

As years passed, I gained experience in the field of gear manufacturing, rather than writing. The call to write wasn't forgotten, it is just that I continued to be haunted by the feeling that I lacked the depth of education to be really good at it. Everything I wrote seemed to be so amateur. Even when re-reading the Nostradamus manuscript, I felt the flow was choppy, and overall not that good. Even worse, I seemed to lack insight on how to improve.

At some point I had an epiphany that one of the most effective writers of old was Paul the Apostle, and he was educated. He had been trained by Gamaliel who is respected by Jews even today. Of course, once educated, Paul went on to write many of the books of the New Testament, and became influential even to the point of surpassing the fame of his teacher. Thus it seems the value of Paul's education was great, and one could argue that the impact of his writing far exceeded the impact of his preaching.

Of course, I already had some education, and had a couple of business writing classes behind me. But in the past I felt that I hadn't paid enough attention because writing seemed like hard work, and I lacked passion for it. But now, the passion was there. So I began to feel that if God was calling me, I had better do something to get back on track.

Therefore, in the year 2000 I began praying about completing a college degree, and decided to check into a number of schools, My brother-in-law suggested Cardinal Stritch – a Catholic school where he had gone – but after some research, there were two other Christian schools with Rockford area extensions that also seemed appealing, along with a couple of schools like North Central that would require major life changes to relocate. The result was that I wasn't reaching a decision. Furthermore, I wanted to be led by God, and I wasn't even sure that God was calling me to go back to school.

One evening, when I attended a church board meeting at Riverside Assembly, a board member looked out the window and spotted a cardinal. Pastor Moore became excited and ran to the window, but the bird had already flown away. Then he explained that he had lived in Rockford for more than ten years and had never yet seen a cardinal. He added that it seemed like everyone else was seeing them, but not him. I thought to myself, "I wish I had prayed for a sign that very day, for then I would be able to claim this as a sign to attend Cardinal Stritch!" But such was not the case, and I couldn't bring myself to make such a life-changing decision on such scanty evidence.

However, the episode did cause me to begin to pray more earnestly for a sign. Several weeks went by. Then one day everything seemed to come to a head. While working I prayed specifically that God would give me three signs before midnight to reveal which school he might want me to attend, if any. I felt that one sign could be a coincidence, but three would give me confidence that God was speaking. And then, just to prove I was serious, I decided that if I did not receive three signs that day, that I would interpret that in itself to be a sign that it was not God's will for me to go back to school, and I would no longer seek a sign. The truth is, I was becoming frustrated not knowing my future and I wanted some kind of closure to the decision making process.

A few hours later as I drove home, there was a song on the local Christian radio station. Suddenly, inexplicably I felt that the next line of the song would contain a sign from God. So I listened intently. The line in the song mentioned two things – fire and blood. As I pondered their meanings, I was able to almost immediately connect the word "blood" with Cardinal Stritch University, since the word "cardinal" and "cardiac" have the same root, and relate to the color red. But I had no clue how the word "fire" might apply. After I got home, I went on the Internet and began checking out each college on my list. But only Cardinal Stritch seemed to connect with fire, for I then saw that the school logo was an oil lamp with a flame! So I decided both words could point to Cardinal Stritch, and there seemed no such connection to any of the other schools. But that still left one more sign unfulfilled.

As it happened, this day was a Tuesday, and that evening was again the next monthly board meeting at our church. During the course of the meeting, our pastor once again looked out the window. Only this time he announced that he was actually looking at the very first Cardinal that he had ever seen since moving to Rockford! So this became my third sign. I bit my tongue and said nothing at the time, but when I returned home I announced rather excitedly that I was enrolling at Cardinal Stritch University.

My new resolve caused me to promptly contact the school and sign up for its Business Administration program. The coursework emphasized writing, and even though the school was Catholic, I found that its professors claimed many different philosophies. Paul Leisure was their writing instructor, and I took several of his classes over  several years. He also did the Community Calendar episodes at our local Christian radio station, and he shared my worldview. He also took a personal interest in my writing, critiqued the rough draft of my "Amazing Evidence" book, and helped me improve it significantly. So I was beginning to see why God had led me to Cardinal Stritch.

It took a lot of hard work, but after four years of classes, a wannabe writer graduated with much more writing experience thanks to the creativity of an amazing God who was able to connect a school's identity with fire, blood, and a little red bird.

Gifts Received

While I was attending school at Cardinal Stritch, we received a brand new 2003 Dodge Caravan as a gift from Brenda's aunt. It was an answer to prayer that took a long time to materialize. It was not the only gift that Aunt Betty gave us. For years we had used a 13-inch television that was actually a vintage computer monitor from the days of Atari and Commodore. By connecting it to a VCR's output, it became a color television. I was okay with that, because I have always had a love-hate relationship with television anyway. But Brenda had been hoping for something better.

One day, as we shopped in Walmart, some large TVs were on display in the main aisle. Brenda mentioned that we could buy one on credit, since money was tight. I suggested that we pray for one, and avoid going further into debt. Brenda agreed, and we both silently agreed in prayer for a new television.

Within a week or so, Aunt Betty also saw the same display and was apparently led by God to buy one for us – the same exact one that we had been looking at! It had an extra large screen by the standards of the day, and was more importantly a welcome answer to prayer – at least for Brenda! Maybe God does actually approve of television??

* * *

CHAPTER 19

We Hear from God

Teaching Sunday school was rewarding on many levels, but also required a lot of work. I usually spent at least eight hours preparing a lesson. Also, during these years I ran sound for services and events, worked with Sonlight and Royal Rangers, and served on the board. At times I felt quite stretched, but a word from God would soon bring a big change.

One Sunday morning Pastor Moore preached a sermon on the topic of "getting out of the rut." After church I remarked to Brenda that I thought I had heard from God. Brenda said, "So did I!" Remarkably, neither one of us, in my memory, had ever made such a statement after a church service.

Brenda asked me what I had heard, so I told her that I thought God was calling me to write a book about evidence for faith. Fifteen years had passed since my first attempt at writing a book. I then followed that up by telling her that I couldn't see how to free up enough time to write.

So then Brenda said she had a solution. The message she thought she heard from God was that he was telling her we needed to switch churches to help my dad with the church he was trying to help get established. It was a major move for us that caused us to feel both some sadness as we left behind friends, and also excitement as we embraced new opportunities. And for us, the move became a major milestone in our spiritual journeys.

Amazing Evidence

For the next several years I worked on writing the book, "Amazing Evidence: Grounds for Belief." Part of the focus of the book was evidence of the Red Sea crossing site, and the location of the real Mount Sinai at Jabal Al Lawz in Saudi Arabia. As a result of my research, I read books and watched videos by people who had unearthed some of this evidence. This left me feeling somewhat unsettled, for it seemed all of the people who had written about the subject were explorers who had major discoveries, while I had nothing to add to the discussion. So one day I prayed and asked God if he would allow me to discover something that I could use in the book. I then recall ending my prayer by saying, "Like that would be possible, because I am stuck here in Illinois."

A couple of days later, on February 21, 2008 to be exact, our son Justin was helping me document artifacts around what we believe is the real site of Mount Sinai in Saudi Arabia. We were doing this by looking at satellite images in Google Earth, when Justin scrolled past something that looked like a skeleton. We were both a little startled. It had already passed from the screen, so he quickly scrolled back to it. That began a process of investigating this object. It measured about the size of a football field, and looked like it might have had a tail that stretched for one third of a mile. After a couple of days, we decided it could be the Biblical sea serpent, Leviathan, which the Bible describes as having been killed in "the wilderness." Since the wilderness is the area where the children of Israel wandered, it made sense that it might be found at the foot of Mount Sinai.

Over the next couple of years we were able to accumulate a substantial amount of evidence from Levitical traditions that this might indeed be the skeleton of Leviathan. I also created three dimensional images of the skeleton by paying to have a satellite take a picture of it from a different angle, and it certainly looks skeleton-like, even in 3D.

Then, Justin took a trip to Israel. In Israel, his tour

104

took him to Zippori where there was an ancient tile floor. His guide pointed out an image of a fire-breathing Leviathan swimming in the Red Sea, which would place it about twenty miles from the location of the object we found. Justin took digital photos of the floor, one of which I subsequently included in that book, and now here. The tile floor also shows a tower on the edge of the Red Sea, that looks remarkably similar to the ones Ron Wyatt found on each side of the Gulf of Aqaba, where Wyatt proposed the Rea Sea crossing actually took place. So the tile floor became another piece of previously unknown evidence, both for our skeleton, and also for Ron Wyatt's proposed location of the Red Sea crossing site. So in answer to prayer, we found something that may indeed prove to be a discovery. Only time will tell for sure.

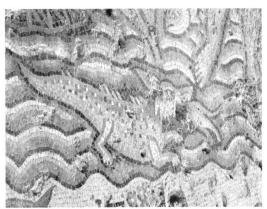

This tile floor at Zippori shows a fire-breathing Leviathan playing in the Red Sea near Mount Sinai. Photo by Justin Hatch.

Skeleton-like object as it appears in Google Earth. It is about the size of a football field. Placing this image next to one taken from a different angle creates a 3D image, in which it can be seen that this object lies above ground level, and appears hollow beneath the torso. Notice the shadow on the far side of the object. A semi truck at the same scale inside the black inset square reveals how huge the object is. (Google Earth coordinates 28.5637N, 35.2808E).

Prayer Moves a U-Haul

Faith Community Church was our new church, and I was working hard on the book. Yet there was still time for helping a member move. When the day for the move arrived, a blizzard had dumped a lot of snow. We managed to fill a large U-Haul truck, but when we tried to drive away, the truck was stuck. Everyone pushed, and we rocked it, yet still it wasn't going anywhere. Then one of the guys suggested we pray, so we all gathered around.

As as we finished praying, a pickup truck stopped and asked if we needed help. They lived a few blocks away, and amazingly had also rented the same size U-Haul truck, which had also been stuck in the snow. So when they saw ours they thought we were probably stuck also. With their fresh experience, pulling ours out was quick and easy. So God lined up experienced help, then led them down our street when we finally gave up on our own efforts and got desperate enough to pray!

* * *

107

CHAPTER 20

Did he say Janitor?

Late one Saturday evening, I was reading the book, *Hand Me Another Brick*, by Chuck Swindoll. At one point he said it was important to have a good attitude doing menial jobs. When I read the words, I was strongly impressed that God was speaking to me directly. More specifically, I thought I heard God say that he had a janitorial type job for me to do at church. It did not sound great to me, but I began more earnestly to pray and read my Bible, and it seemed that I received confirmations that this was true. Though I wasn't excited about it, I surrendered my will and told God I was willing to do whatever he would send my way. The next morning, Pastor Dan Koehler approached me and asked if I would be willing to take on a task that needed to be done at the church.

I thought, "Oh no, here it is!" But I immediately said "Yes," without even asking what it might be. I explained that I was expecting something like this, and said, "maybe you'd better tell me more." The task he was referring to was that of putting together and printing the church bulletin each week. Relieved, I told him that I was all prayed up to clean toilets, so I was actually glad that what God had in mind was a little more appealing than that. Then, for the next couple of years I found colorful public domain pictures to put on the cover, and took pride in printing attractive weekly bulletins. I still have copies of all those bulletins in a couple of notebooks, and enjoy browsing through them from time to time, remembering all the hard work.

In the same church, there was a husband and wife team named Toby and Sandy Moore who were the youth leaders. This was especially significant for our family, because they poured into the lives of two of our sons, Justin and Daniel, even after we moved away. And Justin ended up marrying their daughter Paige, so now they are family!

A Broken Speedometer

Occasionally my younger brother Keith has asked me to help with various handyman projects. One such task involved cutting and removing a client's large tree stump. When our chain saw blades failed to reach the middle, I attempted to pull the stump over with our minivan and a chain. It didn't work, but the jolt at the end of the chain somehow damaged the van's speedometer.

In the end we succeeded in removing the stump, but the speedometer was still dead. Money was tight, and I worried that the lack of a speedometer might lead to a speeding ticket. A few days later, I was reading a shopping flier, and noticed a Garmin GPS with a speed display. I wasn't prepared to buy one, so I began to pray for a Garmin.

Meanwhile, the lack of a working speedometer caused us to drive extra slow. But not to worry, a solution was in the works. After a short time, my brother-in-law called and offered us his old Garmin, as he had just received a new one as a gift. I told him it would be an answer to prayer and explained our need. He dropped it in the mail and in a few more days our problem was solved. Now, I don't know why God didn't just fix the van's speedometer in the first place, but I was grateful for the Garmin, and I have never been without one since.

A few months later we took a road trip south, and the original speedometer suddenly began working again. And then, a week after that, it stopped again. And over the next few years it was on again and off again. But thanks to Ed's response to God's gentle leading, we always knew our speed.

109

Guardian Angels

Brenda works the night shift, and commutes about thirty miles each way. This has led to three deer encounters in the past twenty years. I credit her guardian angels with keeping her from injury. Her latest encounter provided the most direct evidence yet that God wanted us to know that he sent angels to protect her.

It happened late at night. Brenda was driving to work when a deer ran in front of the car. After braking hard, Brenda struck it lightly. She promptly called my phone and told me about it. Her voice was shaky and emotional, and I thanked God that she had not been hurt. But there is more to the story.

Brenda did not think she hit the deer, but video from the dash cam suggests otherwise. In the video, Brenda is singing along with the radio, a fact she is not proud of. The song ends, and out of nowhere a deer runs across. As it passes the left front corner of the car you hear a "thump."

So what does that have to do with an angel you ask? The very next thing in the video is a female voice that says, "I love living independently at home, but sometimes I need a little help. That's when it's nice to know I have an angel by my side." It was a commercial for "Visiting Angels" caregivers, and it is as though God wanted to let us know us that Brenda had an angel by her side!

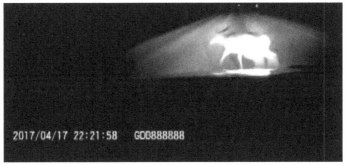

The dash cam image a moment before impact.

Before this encounter Brenda also had a couple other deer encounters. In her first one, she didn't hit the deer – rather it hit her. It was a big buck that first struck the left front fender, then incredibly bounced past the driver's door and struck the van's sliding door. Both the fender and door were seriously damaged, while the driver's door was as good as new! Not so with the deer, for it died, but we were thankful Brenda was not hurt.

Afterward, the van was ugly. We drove it for a long time without fixing it. Then one day, apparently God thought it was time to stop procrastinating. As I was driving to work a car went through a stop sign and smashed the driver's door, damaging only that door! I was shaken, but not injured, but now the fender and both doors on that side were trashed. Thankfully, there was no frame damage. It is as though God has a sense of humor – or that he wanted us to upgrade our image!

The teen girl who hit the van had no insurance, and we didn't make her pay, for who would have believed that the one door she hit had been in perfect condition, when the fender and other door were trashed. But now, we finally got the repairs done.

* * *

*

CHAPTER 21

God Speaks to a Little Girl

My sister, Karen Delaporte, tells a faith story that involves her daughter – our niece – and a haunted house. The haunted house incident occurred in the 1990s, while the story wraps up more recently, in sync with the time-line of this book. Brenda and I experienced the haunted house event after Karen, and her husband Ed, invited us to go through a haunted house with them. But I will let Karen tell the story. Karen posted this account online in a forum under the pseudonym, "Katie Delap." She has granted permission for it to appear in this book, so here it is, in Karen's own words.

One morning the weekend before Halloween my 13-year-old daughter came up to me and said "Mom, today I'm going to meet the man I will marry!" "How could you possibly know that?" I asked this daughter, who had never been boy-crazy like her girlfriends nor ever had a boyfriend or date. She answered matter of factly, "Because I've been asking and asking God who I would end up marrying, and this morning when I was praying, he told me I would meet my future husband today!"

Needless to say, fear struck my heart. My impressionable daughter believing this crazy idea would make for an interesting – if not scary – day. Today, I would definitely keep her close to me and keep a strict eye on her! That night I knew we had plans to take my daughter and her friends to a haunted house. I asked her if she thought she was going to marry one of her friends. She said "No, I'm sure it will be someone totally new that I've never met before." Yikes – fear again.

Nothing eventful happened all day. But that evening

the line waiting to go into the haunted house went down the street and around the block. The kids didn't seem to mind the long wait and goofed around in line and talked to others nearby. I kept a very close eye on my extremely attractive daughter. Come on, I AM her mom, but others think her attractive too. I suspiciously eyed every boy who talked to her!

Finally, our group of teens got to enter. I was behind the group & directly behind my daughter. The long walk was dark, scary, and fun, and took us through pitch-black, winding corridors. Suddenly a man dressed as the Grim Reaper jumped out right in front of my daughter and scared her so badly she screamed and fell backwards - on top of me and those behind me - toppling all of us over! The now kind and sorry Grim Reaper helped us all up, and, noting her extreme reaction of fear, he came out of character long enough to offer to sneak us out a side exit. She said 'no, its okay' and we moved on - embarrassed.

That night my daughter was SO disappointed when she said "I was so sure God told me I would meet him TODAY." Fast forward 10 years. My daughter was the maid of honor for her best friend's wedding and gave a beautiful toast and prayer at the wedding. One of the men attending the groom was from out-of-state and took an interest in my daughter, emailing and calling her after the wedding. Eventually they engaged and married.

After they were married, we were sitting around talking and the subject of haunted houses came up. My son-in-law said he had once helped construct one in an old grocery store building when he spent a year in our town. "Really?" "Yes," he said, and I got to be the Grim Reaper for it and carry a fake scythe!" Comparing notes, they figured out that the exact year he had spent in our city was the year my daughter was thirteen! When asked if he remembered an incident at the haunted house with a frightened girl, he wasn't sure – as all young girls scream. But when he heard she toppled me & others over and he came out of character to offer assistance out a side exit, then he said, "That was you?!? But that was just a little girl I offered help! Usually I pride myself in never coming out of character, but she was so scared and I worried people might have fallen and gotten hurt!" So funny! Yes, a 13-year-old 5-foot girl to a 6 foot 2 inch 19-year-old young man IS 'just a little girl,' as it should be! So my daughter did, indeed, meet her future husband that day. Amazing! Out of the mouth of Babes...! They have been married now for almost 13 years and have 5 children.

So God came through for Sarah, and then allowed her to be so startled that he created a memorable moment so this story could eventually become a small gift of faith! Brenda and I, of course, have close relationships with the individuals in the story. I recall that the haunted house was a church based event, and we were handed Gospel tracts as we left. I also remember Sarah complaining as we left that they shouldn't make haunted houses so realistic!

* * *

*

CHAPTER 22

You will dance again

Health can be complicated. At the age of 40, in the year 1995, I had begun to experience health problems that are not typical for someone so young, and wound up in the emergency room with a Transient Ischemic Attack, or TIA. It was a small short-lived stroke that caused me to go partially blind in one eye and to lose strength in my left arm. The effect was temporary, but scary. It was also a wakeup call, and I began to research health in greater depth. Unfortunately, some of my early efforts were ill-advised, and I continued to experience cardiovascular events for more than a decade.

One day when I was at work I lost strength in my left leg, became dizzy, and struggled to stay standing. The effect continued and I became more and more fearful that I was having a major stroke. As I attempted to walk down the main aisle, I tried to look normal, but was tempted to panic. I asked God, "Am I dying?" Almost immediately, as if in direct answer to my question, I heard words on a nearby radio that said, "You will live, and love, and dance again." The words immediately gave me peace as I sensed God had spoken them to me personally. Of course, time proved the words right – except for the dancing part. I continued to struggle with related health issues for the next decade. And then, finally, healing came.

As I grew older the dizzy spells, numbness, and weakness episodes worsened in frequency to several times a day. One day, I made an appointment to be seen by a doctor, who then made an appointment for me to take a tilt-table test. But before I took the test, I answered an altar call at my dad's church, where we were now attending. People prayed for me, and I asked God for healing. Then, as I was leaving the sanctuary, my dad, who was a pastor at the church, approached me. He knew of my struggles and offered some advice. He simply said, "I think you should lay off the diet sodas." It was true that I was drinking diet Cokes for nearly every meal, and often in-between. I reasoned that this was not the problem, but because I had just finished praying for healing, I took this as though God were speaking through my dad. I immediately stopped the diet drinks, and my symptoms also immediately stopped.

When it came time to take the tilt-table test, I told the doctor that I was no longer experiencing symptoms. He replied that I would therefore probably pass the test. But I did not. During the test I had to stand up for 45 minutes without fainting. When I took the test they strapped me to a tilting table so that if I fainted I could be immediately revived by leaning the table horizontal. After 15 minutes I became nauseous. Then the next thing I knew, they had tilted the table back, and they were telling me I had lost consciousness. As a result, my doctor gave me a prescription.

I was not too excited about taking the prescription, and never did pick it up. Instead, I simply avoided carbonated drinks in general. Now, I still seem sensitive to diet sodas in excess, although I can get away with them once in awhile.

House Judgment

Raising kids can be expensive, and Brenda and I took a course on real estate investing. We used our new-found knowledge to invest in a house, and we helped the owner avoid foreclosure in the process. In the end we made a sizable profit which we split 50/50 with the owner. Of course, then we were ready to do it again. This time, we used the profits to buy a house outright, but a short time later the housing market collapsed and we were left with more debt than we could manage. In all honesty, I ignored signs suggesting we should not have bought this second house, but I trusted my own judgment and felt desperate to pay bills, so we pushed ahead.

Our house and garage two days after we vacated the premises of our home. My sister-in-law Tina and our son Daniel are seen surveying the damage.

At the same time, the following recession resulted in my work hours being cut. The result was that our main residence fell into foreclosure. During the next two and one-half years, we tried everything to catch up and restore our good-standing with the mortgage company, but the mortgage company utilized a variety of schemes to add outrageous lawyer's fees to our debt at a monthly rate that far exceeded our monthly house payment. Ultimately, we failed to get out of foreclosure, a fate that many experienced during those years.

Because we believed the mortgage company was acting unethically, we prayed that God would judge them for their greed, and I also asked friends, family, and our pastors to pray that God would judge them. Finally, the day came when we were told to vacate the premises. I then canceled insurance and signed papers to turn over the house.

But the story doesn't end there. Thirty six hours after

everything was finalized, a storm blew through the area and seriously damaged the house. It appeared to me that three trees fell on the house. A maple tree from the south fell on the garage, an elm tree fell from the north fell onto the back bedroom, and a walnut tree from the house's own back yard fell onto the family room. The trees knocked the garage off its foundation, and dropped a massive branch through the family room roof. In other words, the damage was extensive. Incredibly, it appeared we were the only house in the neighborhood with serious damage. We felt very thankful that we were not in the house when it happened, and also that we no longer owned it.

And that was only the beginning of woes for our mortgage company. Lisa Madigan is our state's Attorney General. During the foreclosure process, I wrote a letter to her detailing how we were being mistreated by our mortgage company. She wrote back saying she was going to do something about it. In the midst of my chaos, I regret failing to send her the additional documentation that she requested, and really doubted she could do anything anyway. Yet she proved me wrong, because she actually did something. *In the end she won a multi-billion dollar settlement against CitiGroup which owned Citimortgage, our mortgage company.* The settlement, along with her name, made national news headlines, which is where I first heard of it. As a result, we were issued a sizable check. This check was enough for us to purchase a used Prius outright, which at the time saved us about $250 per month in gas, due to our long commutes.

A Yellow Blessing

The Prius was a former yellow taxicab that had reached Chicago's mandatory five year retirement age. On the day we bought it, I taped over holes with aluminum

120

tape, then grabbed cans of yellow spray paint and painted over the tape and Yellow Cab symbols. The job was less than professional, but by blending two shades of yellow the colors actually matched fairly well, and really did not look bad – at least if you admire spray paint and duct tape! For us, the car became a major blessing, and the great mileage motivated us to begin a tradition of driving to find warm weather in January. In fact, we were actually able to drive to Orlando, Florida on $51 of gas at a time when gas was nearly four dollars per gallon!

Our yellow taxicab Prius on the day we brought it home, after a quick spray paint job.

In hindsight, it is easy to see God's hand in all of this, but at the time the changes were scary. When I look back, I see that when we ignored God's direction and things went horribly wrong God somehow brought good from them. Misfortune turned into blessings. The bottom line is that God did indeed judge our mortgage company for their misdeeds, and he also was watching out for our well-being, even though at times we could not see it.

One of the results is that Brenda and I now look at finances differently. Like many others, we have caught Dave Ramsey's vision for debt-free living. So while our experience was embarrassing, we are now more conservative with money.

Prius Miracle

March 6, 2015 brought a bitter cold morning, and the Prius would not start. There was little money for repairs as we had been saving to attend two weddings. One wedding was to be 2,000 miles away in Seattle where our son Justin was to wed Paige, and another was to occur 1,000 miles south in Texas, where our son Jonathan was to wed Kiley. The weddings were only one month apart, and this car problem seemed to threaten the trips. So the car sat in our driveway while I attempted to fix it myself. But after spending a meager 34 dollars on parts it still would not run.

According to my journal, about two weeks passed before I gave up. Late one Saturday, I called the Toyota dealer to arrange a tow. The service department was gone for the weekend, and they advised me to call back Monday. But Monday morning brought a blizzard – not great weather for towing.

As a side note, my journal also reveals a small answer to prayer that has absolutely nothing to do with the Prius. Early that Monday morning, our daughter-in-law-to-be Kiley called us saying she had slid into a ditch on a country road. Although Kiley was a Texas native, she was interning at Life Church in Roscoe, where she met our son.

The blizzard continued, and seven or eight inches had already fallen. We were failing to pull her SUV out of the ditch, even with two vehicles daisy-chained together. It was then that a man with a four-wheel drive stopped and added his vehicle to ours. Her car then came out almost effortlessly – hence the answer to our prayers. We thanked this man, and in talking learned he attended Heritage Baptist. I even thought to myself that we should visit his church someday, but it hasn't happened yet. But now, back to the Prius.

By Tuesday afternoon, the roads were plowed, and I called for a tow. *And then an amazing thing happened. While I was still on the phone with Toyota, Brenda announced we had just received a check in the mail for $580.* It was part of a class action settlement that we had signed up for during the previous summer, and one that had nothing to do with the house. We had no idea how large the settlement might be, and we had completely forgotten about it. But that is not the end of the story.

A couple hours later, a tow truck took the Prius to the Toyota dealership. Two days later we had the car back for a total cost of $546 – less than the check in the mail, But when you add that to what my journal says I spent on parts, we were almost exactly even. God's provision and timing were perfect, and we were spared having to dip into our trip savings.

Brenda Safe, Jeep Miracle

Since we moved to rural Wisconsin, Brenda has continued to work the late shift at UPS, commuting thirty miles each way on work days. I often worry about her driving in the middle of the night over snowy roads. On more than one occasion she has been nearly stranded during blizzards when driving the Prius, which sat so low that it often dragged its underside on snow that other cars had already passed over. So a topic of our prayers became a request for an all-wheel drive vehicle.

One evening after Brenda left for work she called me, sounding panic stricken. She told me that she had just been rear-ended while sitting at a stoplight. I immediately borrowed a car and went to get her.

When I arrived, I found that the back left fender of the Prius was digging into the tire, three doors were jammed shut, and the rear hatch wouldn't latch because the rear bumper had been pushed in several inches. As a result, the rear fenders were also bulging out. The good news is that we were able to drive the car home with the fender rubbing the tire after some serious prying with a tire iron.

The other driver's insurance agent totaled the car out and offered us a check. Then, for a little less money they let us keep the Prius. After putting on my "Red Green" hat I was able to stretch the frame to nearly original dimensions with the help of a tree and a chain. This fixed the doors and even the bulging fenders. Only the rear hatch still had problems – it wouldn't latch. But it actually didn't look bad, and creative use of a bundy cord inside the car kept it from bouncing. So the car was like new, at least in my way of thinking. We then went in search of an all-wheel-drive vehicle with what seemed like too little money.

One day on Craigslist I saw a Jeep Cherokee for sale at a local car lot. Brenda was feeling ill, and I am not proud to say that I dragged her out to look at it. After a test drive, we decided to look for something better – and cheaper. So then, without going home, I found another Jeep on Craigslist sixty miles east in Kenosha that seemed like a steal. After emailing the owner, we learned he could show it to us after 6 pm. Knowing bargains don't last long, I am again not proud that I dragged my sick wife along to go look at it. We didn't even take time to stop home, which would eventually come back to haunt us. I then emailed the owner asking for his address.

When we arrived in Kenosha, the owner still hadn't replied, and with no address, things seemed hopeless. Brenda commented that we hadn't even prayed about this, and it certainly seemed like we were paying the consequences. So we stopped at McDonalds and prayed. Then, looking on-line with a smartphone, we found another Jeep well under budget across the state line. It had fewer miles and was five years newer than the one in Kenosha.

After asking God for guidance, we felt we had confirmation that we should look at it. I called the owner to say we could see it the next day because it was already getting late, but he told us we were only 20 minutes from his house. So even though it was late, we headed over to see it. After a test drive we made an offer and bought it.

By then we were really tired, and we didn't want to drive back home in the dark over strange roads. So we checked in at a nearby motel. Of course, we had never packed for such a stay! In the end it seemed worth it, and the next day Brenda was feeling better. The drive home was sunny and pleasant, and the Jeep, with only minor repairs has proven itself dependable. Since then it has been the vehicle of choice in blizzards. So now, in answer to prayer, we had two cars – a Prius with great gas mileage, and a Jeep that goes through snow.

My take-away is that God does not always do things the way we would want him to. In the end, God answered our prayer for a four wheel drive in a dramatic fashion with a collision. Then, we almost blew our search by not praying, but God still led us to a good outcome.

Trust in the name of Jesus

We continued to drive the damaged Prius, which really didn't look that bad after my amateur repairs. But I never was able to make the hatch work properly. Then, in January of 2016, Brenda and I planned a vacation to Florida to get away from the cold.

When our neighbor Michelle learned of our plans, she told us she was praying God would bless us with us a new car because, she informed us on several occasions that the Prius was "on its last legs. " But we didn't pay much attention to Michelle's worries since the car was running fine. I recall once chuckling and saying, "I second that prayer for a new car," assuming of course that if God answered her prayer it would be free!

In nearly 34 years of marriage Brenda and I had never made car payments. As you may recall, even the Prius was a cash purchase, and its great mileage encouraged us to take more trips. We had already driven it to Colorado, Florida, Washington State, and Texas twice. Now, with the odometer nearing 325,000, there seemed to be no end in sight. But Michelle continued to worry.

On the morning we left for Florida, it was twelve degrees above zero, but we weren't fazed because we were heading straight south into warmer weather. We took the long way, wrapping around the Gulf coast through Louisiana and Alabama. As we approached Tallahassee, however, Michelle's worries were realized, and the car quit. We ended up stranded beside the expressway in the shade of an overpass for about two hours in wonderful 75 degree January temparatures. Finally, we were able to get the car towed to the nearest Toyota dealer in Tallahassee. It was Sunday, and the dealer was closed, so the tow truck driver dropped us at a close motel.

The next day was January 16, 2017. The dealer reported that their technicians failed to find a simple solution, and the car probably needed major repairs. We were feeling desperate, and hurried, and were not cash rich. So we began talking options. We couldn't afford to buy another vehicle outright, and if we had to make a down payment, it would cut our vacation short. And that is why we ended up with a brand new Corolla. You see, Toyota had a special no-money-down offer for new Corollas.

As we sat at the salesman's desk, I entered the anticipated payments and insurance into my checkbook app. It was worrisome. Money would be tight if we signed – or so we thought, and just as we were trying to get out of debt. So we were hesitating. I said to Brenda, "What else can we do?"

At that exact moment the news channel on the big screen behind the salesman zoomed in on a street protester's sign which said, "TRUST IN THE NAME OF JESUS." I said to Brenda, "Did you see that?" She had not, so I told her what I saw and said that I was now okay with signing the papers.

We then went on to enjoy a warm and wonderful week in Daytona Beach with a new car, while Wisconsin suffered in a deep freeze. Immediately upon returning home, God came through for us. A long-time employee at my company left for another job. The result was that my very next paycheck increased due to more hours. The increase was more than enough to offset the extra monthly payment, and it has remained so. A few months later, I even began routinely working overtime, after our company was bought out by Seraph Industries, as described earlier in Chapter 16.

Indeed, Michelle's prayer was answered, and God did it without us even having to initiate a car search. In the end, the only necessary decision was to trust in the name of Jesus!

* * *

*

CHAPTER 23

A Prophetic Dream

One winter evening in 2012, I asked God if he could give me a prophetic dream to bolster my faith because I had just read a story of a prophet in the Old Testament that had caused me to seriously doubt whether it really happened. In hindsight my request seems a bit selfish because other than my lack of faith there was no real need to meet. Yet I still prayed passionately because I felt skepticism creeping in, and I didn't like that. So after making the request, I fell off to sleep.

Shortly before waking, I had a vivid dream. In the dream I was driving a snowmobile in a field, and Brenda was sitting behind me. At one point we stopped and gazed at the back of a ranch style house that looked like ours, except this house was white, while ours was dark blue. After a short pause, we rode in a large oval circuit in the field and came around again. At the same place we again stopped and looked at the house. Only this time I noticed that the patio door blinds were now closed and swinging, as though someone had just closed them. Suddenly I felt embarrassed because I realized that the people living there must have noticed me staring on the previous pass, and closed the blinds. Then I woke up. I immediately mentioned to Brenda that I had just had a vivid dream, and that I had prayed for a prophetic dream, but this one certainly didn't seem prophetic. In fact, I have never even ridden on a snowmobile.

About a week or two later, I was working on my laptop computer by our patio doors at dusk. It was getting dark in the house, and I hadn't turned on any lights yet. Enough time had passed that I had all but forgotten about the dream. It was then that a snowmobile with a driver and rider appeared in the field behind the house. They swung around and stopped. It seemed to me that they were staring at me. I assumed they could see everything, including my laptop computer and our television. I wondered why they were staring, and I thought they might be tempted to steal something. So when they left I closed the blinds and went to look out the kitchen window. I didn't expect the snowmobile to return, but they swung around and stopped again in the same place. It was then that I noticed that the blinds were still swinging from having been closed, and realized that the riders were seeing that also, which made me wish I hadn't closed them. Then the riders left, and did not return. And it was only then, at that moment, that I remembered my dream and realized it had just been fulfilled in every detail, except in reality our house was dark blue while in the dream it was white! Otherwise, even the terrain was the same, the path the snowmobile followed was the same, and the swinging of the blinds was the same. I had just experienced the fulfillment of the dream from a totally different perspective.

As a result of the dream, I now gained a new understanding. I now believed that the snowmobile riders had not seen me sitting at the table, nor seen the laptop or TV, nor had it occurred to them they might be invading our privacy. On the second trip, when they noticed the swinging blinds they probably then experienced the same embarrassment that I had known in the dream.

In the end, I understood that God had answered my request for a prophetic dream, but I also realized that God was apparently not calling me to be a prophet or he would have given me a dream with more significance for others. The lesson I learned is simply to not doubt that God is able to communicate to us, and it is my job to simply trust that he will reveal what we need to know when the time is right.

A Provable Prophetic Dream

More recently, I experienced another prophetic dream indirectly. Even though it was not my dream, I like it because it is something that anyone can verify. In other words, anyone reading this can prove its truth with the help of the Internet. For me it became a small gift of faith, and I include it here because I believe it can also become a gift of faith for others.

On April 25, 2018, I stumbled upon a YouTube video only a few hours after it was posted. In the course of the video, the man who posted it said, "Last night ... I prayed to God, 'Give me a dream, something that I can share with everybody.'" Then he went on to say he dreamed a vivid and memorable dream. The video-maker then opened with a simple prayer and shared a couple of Bible verses, followed by some other unrelated ramblings – I am not trying to be harsh, it is just that he likes to ramble. He then began to talk about the dream, which I quote in part here:

> "Okay, I am going to tell you about the dream I had. Alright, I went to work and I was at work on time. I was just doing some odd jobs, and I suddenly realized that I forgot to clock in. So I went over to clock in, and the thing wouldn't let me clock in.... But then I just felt like God put something on me, and I fell to my knees and I just started crying out to people that things were happening – like things were happening right then and there. And I was telling people there were earthquakes, and there were all these gas lines rupturing – bursting – and causing fires all over. But the thing with those gas lines rupturing – they weren't, or at least they said they weren't caused by earthquakes. And it was happening all over that these

gas lines were bursting. And for some reason I got Wisconsin in my head, but maybe that was because of that drill that they're doing, I don't know."

And then he went on to describe other aspects of the dream that don't seem to relate to this part. Then finally he told us that he felt compelled to share the dream.

A Dream, A Message and Some Predictions...April 25th 2018 1:00 pm

2,277 views   👍 71   👎 9   ↗ SHARE   ⇤   ...

To Those Who Will Listen
Published on Apr 25, 2018   SUBSCRIBED 19K 🔔

Let the Holy Spirit touch you and reveal what God wants you to know...I don't know if this will mean anything to anyone, but I felt compelled to share....I really feel that something is going to happen soon, and Jesus will return soon....God

SHOW MORE

After watching the video, I really didn't know what to make of it, and promptly forgot most of it. But then, *the very next day, on April 26, a gasoline refinery in Wisconsin experienced a series of major explosions,* shaking the ground for miles around, and injuring many. On the day after that, the author of the video posted another video stating how *two* parts of that dream had been fulfilled, for there were gas explosions in Wisconsin, and also the time clock where he worked indeed did not work the next day, which was uniquely something that had not happened for many months prior to that. So for those who wish to investigate further, the title of the video on Youtube was, "A Dream, A Message and Some

Predictions," and it was posted on the channel, "To Those Who Will Listen." This video was the first time I had watched one of his videos.

Since this initial fulfillment of the dream, it also seems that a history-making series of gas explosions occurred in the northeastern United States, with explosions striking dozens of homes. The cause of these explosions has now been attributed to extreme pressure buildup in the gas lines. While occurring nearly five months after the video was posted, the scale of these explosions and their unique nature also seems to suggest a possible connection with the dream.

I relate this story here because not only did this person experience a prophetic dream, but I experienced it also, since God allowed me to watch the video before the dream was fulfilled, thus increasing my faith also. Again, it is not very often that you can document something supernatural with hard facts, so here is a video that anyone can watch on YouTube to increase their faith, and anyone can search out the news accounts of the explosions. After all, don't we all struggle at times with the balance between skepticism and faith?

* * *

*

CHAPTER 24

A Call to Switch Churches

When Brenda and I moved to Beloit, we attended a couple of churches for brief periods of time before we settled on Central Christian Church. We went there for several years, until God led us to where we are now. This is how our most recent move happened.

Not long after we moved to Beloit, Brenda and I were leaving a store when we passed an elderly woman trying to start her stalled car in a parking lot. I offered to jump it, and soon she was on her way. But before she left I gave her our cellphone number, just in case she didn't make it home.

A short time later she did indeed call, telling us that she was once again stranded. By the time we arrived at her car, a nearby resident had seen her predicament and was already jump starting her car. We then struck up a conversation and learned that the neighbor was a Christian. He invited us to attend his church – Family Worship Center – which we had often talked about visiting when we would drive past it in Beloit. The neighbor's name was "Hallie," which was both unusual and memorable. But several years passed, and we didn't visit his church, for we were happy with Central Christian. That church is quite large, and has contemporary Saturday services that fit Brenda's work schedule better. It continues to be pastored by David Clark, who coincidentally we crossed paths with recently at a restaurant as I was finishing this book. We loved both his message and his theology – factors I consider important when choosing a church. So we weren't really looking to switch churches.

But God continued to move us toward Family Worship Center. Since moving to Beloit, we had begun attending a small Bible study that meets twice a month in our long-time friends Darrell and Malinda's home. Here, we met Gene and Mary Seger, who have also become good friends. They were also attending Hallie's church, and they also invited us to visit on more than one occasion. But still, we procrastinated. And then, there was another "coincidence" that got our attention.

Family Worship Center was looking for a new pastor, and had just hired a pastor and his wife who lived in Dixon, Illinois. Gene and Mary took a vacation to Branson, Missouri, a few hundred miles south. While there, they attended a large show. During the intermission they became acquainted with the couple sitting next to them, and to their surprise, this couple turned out to be Adam and Amy Meyer, the new pastoral couple for their church, whom they had never met! Indeed, sometimes God works in amazing ways.

I have often said that coincidences show us God loves us, is with us, and wants our attention. Sometimes they can even act as signs that point us to where God is leading. So when Gene and Mary related this event in our small group, it became the coincidence, coupled with the previous invitations, that finally intrigued us enough to actually visit the church. Adam and Amy had not yet arrived, so the first services we attended were led by interim pastor Robert Right, who gave great messages. During one service, I recognized Hallie, the one who had helped the elderly woman, and we re-introduced ourselves. So even before we met the new pastor and his wife, we had already decided to make this our home church simply because it seemed clear that this was where God was leading. And now that we have made the switch, we enjoy Adam's passionate messages, with the anointed worship sessions often led by his wife Amy.

During the following months we got to know Hallie and his wife Tia a little better, which leads us to another twist in this story. One Sunday, Hallie brought his mother-in-law to church. We recognized her because she lives only a a few doors from my parents, about thirty miles south in Rockford, and she would often pray with them. We also knew her casually from years earlier when we had attended the Open Door Mission in Rockford that her husband Rev. Robert Hanserd had run. Brenda and I would meet friends at the mission, and then we would go out street witnessing. Rev. Hanserd had now passed away, but we were struck with how God sometimes lines up relationships to confirm that you are where you belong, at least that is how we felt about these things. I guess in God's eyes it is indeed a small world.

* * *

*

CHAPTER 25

Miracle in a cornfield

A week before labor day in 2016 our son Justin and his wife Paige were visiting from Seattle. I took Monday off work early to spend time with them, and we went mini-putting at Volcano Falls in Rockford. As we finished, a thunderstorm was rolling in.

Brenda then received a text from our neighbors Michelle and Ryland, who were on their way back from Florida with their son. Michelle was calling to say they were stranded in a cornfield about fifty miles south of us near Dixon, Illinois. So we headed out to rescue them.

We drove through a torrential downpour. When we arrived, we found them on Bollman Road, a narrow gravel road about a mile long, with tall corn and deep mud on both shoulders. It was obvious that cars had driven through the mud to get around them.

They told us how they had been making good time on the highway until they came to a roadblock where a cop directed them to leave the highway and turn onto this narrow gravel road. Then they described how traffic was barely moving. It was then that they began to hear a grinding noise. But they kept moving, and soon afterward, the motor died. *When they got out they saw that one end of the gas tank had fallen and was dragging on the gravel. It now had a hole in it that leaked out about twenty gallons of gas, killing the engine.* We all were extremely thankful that the cop had taken them off the highway when he did or it would have been disastrous for them if the tank had dragged on the pavement at sixty miles per hour. This genuinely seemed to be a miracle of divine intervention. But it leaves one question unanswered. Was the cop an angel?

Amazing God

When Brenda and I read and re-read these accounts, we experience a deep sense of gratitude as we recall the times when God stepped in and changed the course of our lives. We know that other Christians also have testimonies like these because we have heard many over the years. Sometimes I wonder if too many take answers to prayer for granted, never record them in a journal, and then forget they ever happened.

So what is the secret then to seeing God work? Probably most Christians would agree there is nothing we can do to force God to do anything. Our part is to simply trust him and place problems in his hands, to pray hard when situations demand it, to ask others to pray hard, and to sometimes be willing to take steps of faith.

I have to wonder, if we never stepped off a few faith cliffs would we ever know if God could catch us? The bottom line is that when an average human being trusts deeply that the God who loves them is in control of every molecule, atom, and quark in the universe, then one can look for and expect little miracles!

The End

* * *

*

*

Proof

Made in the USA
Columbia, SC
08 October 2018